The Touch of God

Rodney M. Howard-Browne D. Min.

R.H.B.E.A. Publications
Louisville, Kentucky

Unless otherwise indicated, all scriptural quotations are from the *King James Version* of the Bible.

The Touch of God
ISBN 0-9583066-9-9
Copyright © 1992 by
Rodney M. Howard-Browne
P.O. Box 197161
Louisville, KY 40259-7161 U.S.A.

Published by
R.H.B.E.A. Publications
P.O. Box 197161 Louisville, KY 40259-7161 U.S.A.
P.O. Box 3900, Randburg 2125 South Africa

Printed in the United States of America

Cover design and book production by
DB & Associates Design Group, Inc.
P.O. Box 52756
Tulsa, OK 74152

Printed in the United States of America.

Dedication

To all those who have gone before us, who God has used in a wonderful way and to the new breed of men and women that God is raising up in these last days that will show forth the Glory of God without sharing the glory.

Contents

Introduction

I felt led of the Lord to write this book on the subject of the anointing. I write not so much from a theoretical but from a practical standpoint about that which has become so real to me, during the past 14 years since the encounter I had with the Holy Spirit in July, 1979.

In July of 1991, during a meeting in San Diego, California, as I was preaching, I found these words coming out of my mouth. The Lord said through the supernatural gift of prophecy, "The great men and women of God that I am using in the earth today are not being used because they are something special. I am using them for one reason and one reason alone. It's because they've touched Me and I have touched them."

Although some people **are** specially gifted and called by God, others may think that those who are being used by Him are His favorites. Yet many don't realize that they pressed in and found a place in God that is special. Anyone who desires to, can press in and touch the hem of His garment. If we can realize this, then we will see that we should not allow spiritual jealousy to come in just because God doesn't use us in the same way He uses others. We must not criticize and be judgmental.

In Acts 5:34-39, we read that even a Pharisee named Gamaliel had enough sense to suggest that the counsel should, "Refrain from these men, and let them alone: for if this counsel or this work be of men, it will come to nought: But if it be of God, ye cannot overthrow it; lest haply ye be found even to fight against God" (Acts 5:38, 39).

I pray the Church would have as much sense as the Pharisee Gamaliel and stop criticizing, thinking that God set them as the watchdog of the Church. I write this book out of a burning desire to see the Church rise up and flow together and stop fighting one another. The time is short and Jesus is coming so very soon. When it's all said and done and we stand before the judgement seat of Christ, we will all have to give account of what we've done for the Lord and not what our brothers or sisters have or have not been doing.

It is important to realize that criticism is the anointing (clothing) of the flesh. It needs to pull others down in order to lift itself up. Humility is the clothing of the spirit. It lays its life down in order to lift others up.

This book will challenge you to a deeper walk with God. It is the desire of my heart to see thousands of ministers rise up in the anointing, with the fire of the Holy Ghost and do the work of the ministry in these last days. I deal with the subject of the anointing and the call of God and many issues that have hindered the move of God and hindered God's servants. Some of what I share will hit hard and might cut away the counterfeit so that we might experience the genuine move of the Spirit.

The subject of the anointing is spoken about by some in a vague way. I trust that throughout this book on the touch of God, as I share with the reader from the Word and some of the experiences I have had, as God has touched me, that there would come a hunger and a thirst for more of God and the things of the Spirit.

In endeavoring to bring forth the genuine move of God and the fruit that will remain, it is my desire that the reader has an understanding of the basics of the anointing and how he or she might be used of God.

This book does not come from a heart that is critical or bitter and it is not my intention to hurt anyone. No names are mentioned and no names are implied so please do not try to read something into what I have written. I felt that I could not write a book that got down to the meat of what I believe the Spirit of God is saying, unless I addressed certain issues.

I do not believe in judging or being critical, but we must speak the truth in love. It is evident in the Gospels that Jesus addressed certain issues and spoke out against the Pharisees and Sadducees and the religious hierarchy of the day. And it is also evident in the writings of the great Apostle Paul that he addressed many issues, warning and bringing correction.

I also realize that some who do not know me personally and know my heart will be critical of some of that which I write. My heart is to see restoration and people who are walking in love, forgiveness, and acceptance. The Word of God declares in Galatians 6:1 that if you see your brother overtaken in a fault, "restore such an one in a spirit of meekness; considering thyself, lest thou also be tempted." I consider myself and judge myself by the very words that I have been prompted by the Spirit of God to write.

Martin Luther said, "Here I stand; I cannot do otherwise, so help me God." As he spoke out in his day, I must speak the truth today. I am tired of non-charismatics or non-Pentecostals, who know nothing of what they are talking about, ripping and tearing apart the Pentecostal and charismatic movement and labeling everyone

a spiritual fruitloop, in their relentless witchhunt to erad-
icate all of the excesses in the movement.

I, as an insider, feel that I can speak firsthand on
these issues. I challenge anyone who reads this book to
prayerfully consider what I believe the Holy Spirit
prompted me to say. I am telling the truth and before
God I lie not. I pray that as you read the pages of this
book that you will come to know what it means in your
life, to have the touch of God.

Rodney M. Howard-Browne
July 1992
Louisville, Kentucky

Chapter 1
Understanding the Anointing

Laying the Foundation

And Jesus returned in the power of the Spirit into Galilee: and there went out a fame of him through all the region round about.

And he taught in their synagogues, being glorified of all.

And he came to Nazareth, where he had been brought up: and, as his custom was, he went into the synagogue on the sabbath day, and stood up for to read.

And there was delivered unto him the book of the prophet Esaias. And when he had opened the book, he found the place where it was written,

The Spirit of the Lord is upon me, because he hath anointed me to preach the gospel to the poor; he hath sent me to heal the brokenhearted, to preach deliverance to the captives, and recovering of sight to the blind, to set at liberty them that are bruised,

To preach the acceptable year of the Lord.

Luke 4:14-19

And great multitudes came together to hear, and to be healed by him of their infirmities.

And he withdrew himself into the wilderness, and prayed.

And it came to pass on a certain day, as he was teaching, that there were Pharisees and doctors of the law sitting by, which were come out of every town of Galilee, and Judea,

1

and Jerusalem: and the power of the Lord was present to
heal them.

Luke 5:15-17

But ye have an unction from the Holy One, and ye
know all things.

1 John 2:20

But the anointing which ye have received of him
abideth in you, and ye need not that any man teach you: but
as the same anointing teacheth you of all things, and is truth,
and in no lie, and even as it hath taught you, ye shall abide
in him.

1 John 2:27

Having an Understanding of the Anointing

It is so important to have an understanding of the
anointing in the day and time that we are living. Many
today do not recognize the power of God. They
wouldn't recognize the anointing if it slapped them in
the head.

People often say, "Oh, the anointing is here," but
when you ask them how they know, they reply, "Well,
it's just here." They don't know any more than that.
Sometimes ministers will make this spiritual statement:
"Brother Rodney more is happening in the supernatural
realm than is happening in the natural realm." That's a
bunch of religious garbage. If it is happening in the
realm of the Spirit, then it will be manifested in the natural realm.

Many do not recognize the anointing. This is evident to me especially when I begin to pray for people in
the meetings. I call all those who sense His presence on
them to come forward. Some come to the front and they
have no anointing of God on them. Others sit in their
seats shaking all over, wondering what is going on.

When I finally call them forward and tell them the power of God is all over them, they say, "Oh, is that what it is?"

What Is the Anointing?

The anointing is not some mystical something out there. The anointing is the presence and power of God manifested. We could say that the anointing is the manifest presence of God.

There is a vast difference between the omnipresence of God and the manifest presence of God. The Lord is omnipresent but He is not manifesting or displaying His power everywhere. When God's power does manifest, something is going to happen. We read in Luke 5:17 that the power of the Lord was present to heal. When God walks in something happens, something takes place. The anointing is tangible. It can be felt. Just as electricity is tangible, so the anointing is tangible.

God's Electricity

We know that electricity has been in existence since the beginning of time, yet it wasn't until Benjamin Franklin and other scientists in experiments discovered certain principles about it that mankind learned to harness it and came to reap the benefits of electricity. The Church has been ignorant of the anointing and how it operates, but it still exists. We can, by the Spirit of God, understand the operation of the anointing and cooperate and flow with the Spirit of God.

It's the same with the light bulb. It could have always been in existence, but it took Thomas Edison several thousand experiments to come across the right substance for the filament in the light bulb to enable it to work. The laws of flight have always been in existence, but it took the Wright brothers to discover how they operated. Today we reap the benefit of what they discovered.

Don't Try to Explain Away the Supernatural

I was reading a Bible commentary of a world-renowned theologian who had taken into his mind to explain away every passage of scripture that contained any reference to the anointing or the supernatural power of God. He said that it was asinine to think that in this day and age the anointing can actually be transferred by the laying on of hands. He had chosen to overlook the supernatural aspect of God's Word.

This is true in many church circles. They deny the power of God from its rightful place and so the youngsters are turning to rock music, drugs, alcohol, and free sex, and the yuppie generation is turning to the New Age movement. There are two reasons for this. One, they have a hunger in their hearts for something that is real. Two, the Church is not meeting or fulfilling their need and instead has become a referral system. Alcoholics and drug addicts are sent to rehabilitation places instead of being set free by the power of the Holy Ghost.

Don't tell me that the anointing of the Lord was in a meeting and nothing happened. You might have a big church, thousands of people, a beautiful robed choir, beautiful chandeliers, clarinet solos, celebrity speakers, and a large television ministry, but without the anointing — the touch of God — you have nothing at all.

Hollywood Hype and a World Wrestling Federation Spirit in the Church

In some meetings being held nowadays, the anointing is as scarce as hen's teeth, as one preacher said. You need a magnifying glass to find it. The anointing is not hype.

In some circles there's a lot of Hollywood. There's a lot of hype. At some meetings, you would think any moment that they would bring on the wrestlers and have a tag team match in the church. They have fleshly preaching, praying, singing, and dancing — a lot of hoopla — but no results.

We live in a day and age of entertainment where people want to come and sit in beautiful, air-conditioned auditoriums and be entertained on a Sunday morning and night. A minister can stand in the pulpit and scream and jump around or can even look dignified and professional, but if the touch of God is not on the minister's life, he can forget it — lives will not be changed.

Are You Tired of Hype?

I have attended some large charismatic meetings where who's who in the charismatic zoo has been present and yet no anointing manifest. It's almost like some are afraid that if the Holy Ghost showed up, they might not know what to do. So rather than display their spiritual ignorance, they would rather close the meeting down or get into some fleshly works program of binding the devil and hyping up a service. Then at least the starving sheep might go from the meeting feeling they were dished up some stale bread.

In some Bible schools, they endeavor to teach how to preach, but in my estimation, that's equivalent to teaching a pig to sing. You can be taught all the theory concerning the art of preaching, but if there is no anointing or touch of God on an individual's life, it will just be hype.

Some even think that shouting is the anointing or being professional in your communicative ability is the anointing. To stir people to emotions will not bring change. God wants fat hearts, not fat heads.

The scripture says, "Not by might, nor by power, but by my spirit, saith the Lord of hosts (Zechariah 4:6). I told the Lord in the first part of my ministry that if He was not going to do anything, I was not going to do anything. He told me that He was waiting on me, not that I was waiting on Him. And He said if I would just give Him an opportunity to move, He would move.

Some Are Afraid to Lose Control

I have seen hosts on Christian television shut down their guests because of fear of losing control of the program. They didn't want to be overshadowed by the anointing on the guest's life. They would rather try to do some religious mumbo jumbo and abort the broadcast because they want control. Some pastors are the same way. They would rather bring evangelists into their church who do a worse job than they do in order that their ministry might look great in the eyes of their people.

These are the games that people play in the church. It's political nonsense that if you want to get into this church or get around this preacher then there are certain things you must or must not do. I purposed in my heart I would rather quit the ministry than play games. No man will tell me where to preach and what to preach. You can't buy me because I am not for sale. Like Paul, I will be a servant to all but a slave to none.

Not By Might Nor By Power

I saw so many preachers killing themselves and losing their families that I decided the price was too high. I told the Lord that I was not going to kill myself or lose my family. The Lord said to me, "Son, you don't have to kill yourself. I already died two thousand years ago. Just walk in the light of what I did two thousand years ago."

I don't do anything in my meetings other than allow the Holy Spirit to come and have free rein. What is so beautiful is that He comes and manifests Himself and touches the lives of individuals in a wonderful way.

It's not our power; it's His. It's not our ability; it's His. He wants us to rely upon Him and trust Him to put us over. Jesus said, "Freely ye have received, freely give" (Matthew 10:8). He said, "Behold, I give unto you power to tread on serpents and scorpions, and over all the power of the enemy" (Luke 10:19).

The Anointing Destroys the Yoke

We have all heard it said that the anointing breaks the yoke, but the scripture actually says that the anointing destroys the yoke.

> And it shall come to pass in that day, that his burden shall be taken away from off thy shoulder, and his yoke from off thy neck, and the yoke shall be destroyed because of the anointing.
>
> **Isaiah 10:27**

If I come into your house and break something, you will be able to glue it back together again. But if I destroy it, you will not be able to fix it up ever again. There is a big difference between a yoke that is broken and a yoke that is destroyed.

When you have a revelation concerning the anointing and the fact that the anointing is the very tangible presence of Almighty God, then even when you are ministering to people who have an incurable disease such as cancer, you will begin to see them healed by the power of God. I call it Holy Ghost chemotherapy or Holy

7

Ghost radiation treatment because when you minister by the tangible anointing, you will find an actual transferring of the anointing.

Go With the Flow

When the presence of God comes into a building, it always comes for a purpose. His presence comes to minister to people to set them free. When His power begins to manifest, those who are ministering need to be sensitive to the flow of the Holy Ghost. If the preacher pushes right on with his own purpose, his own plan, to follow his own agenda for the meeting, then many times the Holy Spirit is grieved and His hands are tied and nothing will happen.

I know many times when I get into the meetings, the Lord will prompt me to go in a different direction than I had planned. When I obey Him and do what He wants done, then lives are touched. Under the anointing, God can do more in two minutes than we can do in months. Oh, that we would wake up and begin to realize what is available to the church! Ministry should not be an occupation or a job, but a new covenant preacher ministering in the power of the resurrected Lord Jesus Christ.

In My Name Cast Out Devils

At one time, I was asked by one of the Bible students at the school where I was lecturing to come and pray for his aunt who was dying of cancer. Doctors had given her up to die. She only had several hours to live.

When I arrived at the hospital room, I saw the lady laying in the bed in a critical condition. I felt prompted to speak out and say, "You spirit of death and cancer, I adjure you by Jesus Christ of Nazareth, the Son of the living God, to come out of this woman."

8

As I said those words, I felt impressed to say it again and again which I did for about 20 minutes. I kept saying, "You spirit of death and cancer, I adjure you by Jesus Christ of Nazareth, the Son of the living God, to come out of this woman. I curse you just as Jesus cursed the fig tree. I curse this cancer."

Something happened so suddenly that one minute it wasn't there, the next minute it was. The power of God hit this woman. It started at the top of her head and then moved down to her feet. Her whole body began to shake until the bed shook. The power of God hit her nephew who was reserved and quiet, and he began to shout. God's power shook this woman right out of bed and she was healed by the power of the Holy Ghost. The next day she went shopping. That's how you really know that a woman is healed!

The Anointing Is the Equipment

The anointing is the supernatural equipment to get the job done. God will never call someone to do something without equipping them with the necessary tools to get the task done. Just like a mountain climber has to have the right boots and equipment, so we, if we would be able ministers of the new covenant, need the anointing.

We could also say that the anointing is the cloak or the mantle, or the clothing. Without it, we are naked. This is what happened to Adam in the Garden of Eden. He was originally clothed in the shekina glory of God. When Adam sinned, he lost his clothing and found out he was naked.

Through the new covenant and the finished work of the cross, Jesus restored back to us what Adam lost in the Garden of Eden. As the scripture says, "We have this treasure in earthen vessels" (Second Corinthians 4:7).

I don't ever want to minister without the anointing of God. Otherwise, whatever is done will be done in my own strength and ability. We cannot fake the anointing. It's either there or it's not there. Many times I will get up in the pulpit prepared to preach and I end up teaching because the anointing to preach is not there. We need to hook up and flow with the anointing of the Holy Spirit if we want to see results.

God's Ability Upon Man

Jesus said, "The Son can do nothing of himself, but what he seeth the Father do" (John 5:19). He said, "I came down from heaven, not to do mine own will, but the will of him that sent me" (John 6:38). The anointing is not based on a man's education or the lack of it. On the contrary, I have seen some very unqualified people minister under the greatest anointing. Sometimes natural ability and talent hinder the individual from being used of God because they are relying on their ability, and not on Him.

God takes the foolish things of the world to confound the wise (First Corinthians 1:27). Not many high and mighty are chosen. The Bible says, "God hath chosen the weak things of the world to confound the things which are mighty; And base things of the world, and things which are despised, hath God chosen, yea, and things which are not, to bring to nought things that are: That no flesh should glory in his presence" (First Corinthians 1:27-29).

It never ceases to amaze me how many think that because they were successful in business they will be successful in the ministry. They tend to forget that it all revolves around the call of God and the touch of God.

The Anointing is Like the Wind

The anointing is not a feeling, but it is felt. It's as if you unscrewed a light bulb and stuck your finger in the socket, you would have a shocking experience. The anointing is not people falling under the power, yet often people can be overcome by the anointing and the phenomenon of people falling under the power may be witnessed. These are the *results* of the anointing in that place.

The anointing is like the wind. You cannot see the wind, but you can see the results when it blows. You cannot see the anointing, but you can see the results. People get saved, healed, set free, and delivered.

I asked the Lord one day why some never sensed His presence. He said it was because many are so caught up in the affairs of this life that their thought life is far from Him. Most of their waking moments are taken up with the things of the natural. They never spend any time in worship or in communication with the Lord. It's almost like they are on another wavelength.

It's like having a radio and wanting to listen to a certain station and then not tuning in to the correct frequency. You'll never pick up the message. If you make the adjustment down in your spirit, suddenly the signal will come through loud and clear.

Chapter 2
The Anointing on the Life and Ministry of Jesus

And Jesus returned in the power of the Spirit into Galilee: and there went out a fame of him through all the region round about.

And he taught in their synagogues, being glorified of all.

And he came to Nazareth, where he had been brought up: and, as his custom was, he went into the synagogue on the sabbath day, and stood up for to read.

And there was delivered unto him the book of the prophet Esaias. And when he had opened the book, he found the place where it was written,

The Spirit of the Lord is upon me, because he hath anointed me to preach the gospel to the poor; he hath sent me to heal the brokenhearted, to preach deliverance to the captives, and recovering of sight to the blind, to set at liberty them that are bruised,

To preach the acceptable year of the Lord.

Luke 4:14-19

It is important that we look at the life and ministry of Jesus to fully understand the operation of the anointing. This will help us understand the words of Jesus when he said, "He that believeth on me, the works that I do shall he do also; and greater works than these shall he do; because I go unto my Father" (John 14:12).

Nothing Jesus did was because He was the Son of God. The Bible says He laid aside His royal robes of

13

deity and when He walked the earth He did so as a prophet under the Abrahamic covenant.

Some speculate and say that as a child, Jesus would heal the animals and that He would walk on water to entertain His friends. But I want you to know that the ministry of Jesus did not begin until He came to the River Jordan and was baptized by John. The Holy Spirit descended like a dove and sat upon Him and God spoke out of heaven and said, "This is my beloved Son, in whom I am well pleased" (Matthew 3:17).

From that moment of time, Jesus was anointed to stand in the place of ministry. We read in the book of Acts 10:38, "How God anointed Jesus of Nazareth with the Holy Ghost and power: who went about doing good, and healing all that were oppressed of the devil; for God was with him."

In Him Dwelt the Fullness of the Godhead Bodily

It is interesting to see the Godhead in operation in this passage of scripture. "How God anointed Jesus with the Holy Ghost." I believe that if we would be used by God, we too would have to be anointed by God. Just as Jesus was anointed, so we need to be able to know the day and the time that the touch of God occurred in our lives.

Jesus stood in every one of the fivefold ministries. The scripture says that because He spoke the Word of God, God gave Him the Spirit without measure (John 3:34).

Jesus Stood in Every One of the Fivefold Ministries

Jesus was an apostle. He came on one of the greatest missionary journeys of all time to the earth to redeem and buy man back. He was a prophet. He said no prophet is without honor except in his own country. He spoke by revelation. He was an evangelist. He brought the evangel — the good news of the gospel. He was a pastor. He was the Good Shepherd. He said a good shepherd gives his life for his sheep. He was a teacher. He taught them as one who had authority and not as the scribes and Pharisees.

You and I do not individually have the ministry of Jesus because He never gave His ministry to one individual. He divided His ministry to the Body.

Ephesians 4:7, 11 says, "But unto every one of us is given grace according to the measure of the gift of Christ. And he gave some, apostles; and some, prophets; and some, evangelists; and some, pastors and teachers."

God Calls and God Anoints

I want you to notice that everyone who stands in a fivefold office collectively makes up the ministry of Jesus on earth today. No man can call, no man can appoint, but it is God Almighty who anoints.

We can safely say that Jesus' ministry was complete and yet isn't it amazing that there are individuals today who sincerely believe that they are the only ones who have anything. In essence, they are saying that there is no one else needed just like them.

I was amused to read the write-up of one individual who billed himself as an apostle and then proceeded to inform the reader why he was an apostle. Then he billed himself as a prophet and then as an evangelist and then as a teacher. The only one he didn't bill himself as was as a pastor. I thought to myself, *If he could get about 50 people to meet every Sunday, he could call himself a pastor.*

The Gospel Doesn't Rest on One
Individual Alone

God does not call one individual to carry the message of the cross and place all of that responsibility on one person. Imagine if every ministry was the same. Wouldn't that be boring? No, He calls all of us. To one He gives the one talent and to another He gives three and to another five. When we are faithful over little, He makes us a ruler over much. (See Matthew 25:14-30.)

You and I have the Spirit by measure, but corporately, we have the Spirit without measure. That's why this last day revival will not come through one single group or denomination. Rather, it will come through a blood-washed church that God will raise up in the hour to show forth His glory, but not share His glory. Many by their attitudes want to share the glory of God. But without Him, without His touch, we are nothing.

No man will be able to get the glory for that which God shall do in these last days. It will be a supernatural outpouring of the Spirit that no one denomination or group can control. The knowledge of the Lord will cover the earth as the waters cover the sea (Isaiah 11:9).

Give Him all the Glory

Jesus said, "And I, if I be lifted up from the earth, will draw all men unto me" (John 12:32). We have to realize that He said if *I* be lifted up. Not Apostle Doodad or Prophet Bucketmouth, but Jesus must be exalted. Always ascribe all praise, all glory, all honor unto His majestic name. He alone is worthy to receive praise.

Chapter 3
The Anointing on Every Believer

Every believer is anointed with the ministry of reconciliation, but not every believer is anointed or equipped to stand in the fivefold ministry offices according to Ephesians 4:7-11. I am not trying to make it hard for the believer to be in the full-time ministry, but I would like the reader to understand that the fivefold ministry does not grow on trees. You cannot buy them down at the supermarket or the five-and-dime store. You cannot raise them up in a Bible school or seminary setting. These gifts are given by God Almighty and come from heaven above and not by the hands of man.

Every believer is anointed when they get born again. God comes and makes His home on the inside of us. The scripture says, "If any man be in Christ, he is a new creature: old things are passed away; behold, all things are become new" (Second Corinthians 5:17). You are set apart.

Old Testament Prophets, Priests, and Kings
New Testament Kings and Priests

Under the Old Covenant, God anointed three groups of people. First, He anointed the prophets, second, the priests, and third, the kings. He would cause His Spirit to rest upon them.

17

Then came the New Covenant. When Jesus cried, "It is finished," the veil of the temple was rent in two from top to bottom. The Holy Spirit came out of an earthly tabernacle made with the hands of man never again to live therein. Now He lives in your heart and my heart. We have become the temple of the living God according to First Corinthians 6:19 and Second Corinthians 6:16.

Every believer can operate in any one of the nine gifts of the Holy Spirit found in First Corinthians 12. God did not say that it was just for the apostles, prophets, evangelists, pastors, and teachers. As the scripture says in First Corinthians 12:7, "The manifestation of the Spirit is given to every man to profit withal."

The fivefold ministry will have a greater manifestation of the nine gifts of the Spirit, with a greater anointing, than the laity.

The Well and the River

In John 4:15, Jesus said, "Whosoever drinketh of the water that I shall give him shall never thirst; but the water that I shall give him shall be in him a well of water springing up into everlasting life." I want you to notice it says a well. The scripture says, "With joy shall ye draw water out of the wells of salvation" (Isaiah 12:3). We could call this first anointing a "well" anointing.

> In the last day, that great day of the feast, Jesus stood and cried, saying, If any man thirst, let him come unto me, and drink.
>
> He that believeth on me, as the scripture hath said, out of his belly shall flow rivers of living water.
>
> (But this spake he of the Spirit, which they that believe on him should receive: for the Holy Ghost was not yet given; because that Jesus was not yet glorified.)
>
> **John 7:37**

In this scripture, we not only see a well, but something that is bigger than a well. We see a river. In other words, you can have a "well" anointing when you get born again, and you can have a "river" anointing when you get the baptism in the Holy Ghost.

Jesus told the disciples to tarry at Jerusalem for the coming of the Holy Spirit. He said in Acts 1:8, "But ye shall receive power, after that the Holy Ghost is come upon you: and ye shall be witnesses."

Power to Be a Witness

We can actually have power to be a witness. The word witness in this scripture means *martyr*. In other words, witnesses are a people who are prepared to die for what they believe. A witness is someone who is radical in his faith and the communication of it. We see this actually portrayed in the life of Peter, the one who denied the Lord. On the day of Pentecost, after receiving the Holy Ghost, he boldly preached and proclaimed the gospel.

This also can be witnessed in the life of Saul of Tarsus who was one of the greatest persecutors of the Christian Church. God turned his life around after his encounter with the Lord on the road to Damascus. Three days later, Saul was endued with power from on high after Ananias came and laid his hands on him. He received his sight and the gift of the Holy Spirit. (See Acts 9:1-18.)

What a change had taken place, what a transformation. And it is all because of the anointing or the touch of God.

The Anointing on the Ministry of Helps

If you are faithful, and follow God's plan for your life, He will put a desire in your heart to be a help in the ministry. God is not looking for pew warmers, but for people who are being used of Him to touch the lives of others through ways other than the fivefold ministry.

> And in those days, when the number of the disciples was multiplied, there arose a murmuring of the Grecians against the Hebrews, because their widows were neglected in the daily ministration.
>
> Then the twelve called the multitude of the disciples unto them, and said, It is not reason that we should leave the word of God, and serve tables.
>
> Wherefore, brethren, look ye out among you seven men of honest report, full of the Holy Ghost and wisdom, whom we may appoint over this business.
>
> But we will give ourselves continually to prayer, and to the ministry of the word.
>
> Acts 6:1-4

The ministry of helps is anything that helps the fivefold ministry get the job done. Out of those seven men who were chosen, we know of only Philip who later became an evangelist. Stephen was a man full of faith and the Holy Ghost and did great wonders and signs among the people. Later he became the first martyr of the Church.

Who Falls into this Category?

Under the category of the helps ministry, we see that this includes psalmists, intercessors, deacons, elders, and others.

The ministry of helps is anything that helps get the job done. We see this in the ministry of Jesus when He fed the five thousand. We find Him instructing the twelve to sit everyone down in groups and then He broke the bread and the fish and He gave it to the disciples. They in turn gave it to the multitudes.

I think that the key to the ministry of helps is that the moment the helps ministry becomes a hindrance it ceases to be the helps ministry anymore. It is a fact that many churches are hindered by their deacon board or elders who don't carry the vision of the pastor and are not a help at all.

I have seen negative incidents arise because of psalmists who think that music is more important than the ministry of the Word. We see them causing problems for the pastor and some even end up splitting the church.

Likewise, deacons who want to control the pastor, instead of holding up his hands just as the hands of Moses were raised, will tie the hands of the pastor. Financial boards or administrators who control the finances as though they were their own, create the same problem. They want to vote on whether or not they should give the pastor an annual raise or the feasibility of supporting missions on a regular basis.

Notice in Acts 6 that the prerequisite for being a deacon is to be a man full of faith and the Holy Spirit. I believe that this goes for all those in the ministry of helps. There is nothing worse than having people in the ministry along with you whom you have to carry. They are a dead weight because they are full of doubt and unbelief. You have probably heard the saying that it is hard to soar like an eagle when you are surrounded by turkeys!

Some are anointed psalmists, intercessors, administrators, deacons and elders, and they are such a blessing when they lift up the hands of the minister and help him to function in that place of ministry. But, oh, what a dead weight they are when they are filled with the negative and cannot see what God has planned. Many that might even have been called to be a check and a balance have ended up being a weight around the neck of the servant of God.

Many an anointed man has fallen because he surrounded himself with people who were not led by the Spirit. Some were just working in the ministry as a job and had no anointing to stand in that place of ministry. They were a hindrance and not a help. Or some were "yes" people that agreed to everything that he said for fear of getting fired. Instead of giving him a warning, they watched as he was led astray out of the plan and the purpose of God for his life and ministry.

Chapter 4

The Fivefold Ministry and the Call of God

When someone is called to the fivefold ministry, that individual doesn't need to constantly tell others of his title or his ministry gift. An orange tree or a lemon tree does not need to grow a sign out of the side of it saying, "I am an orange tree," or "I am a lemon tree." On the contrary, when the season of that fruit arrives, we will eat of the fruit of that tree. So with the ministry gifts. You will know them by their fruit, not by their gifts.

There is a move in this day in which it seems to be very important to have a title. "I am an apostle." "I am a prophet." As if it's so important to be labeled. I believe that God wants to raise up people in these last days who will not have only titles, but have the power of that office. In other words, to function not in name, but in power. We are nothing without Him.

The Apostle

The apostle is a sent one. His ministry seems to embrace every one of the other gifts and might function in them from time to time as God permits. They are individuals who have something that is beyond the ordinary. An apostle is someone who is sent by God on a specific task. They called Smith Wigglesworth an apostle of faith. He led the way to new conquests for Christ.

The Prophet

The prophet is one who speaks by divine inspiration and revelation. This is not one who merely operates in the simple gift of prophecy. There are many who prophesy, but that doesn't make them a prophet. A prophet is either a preacher or teacher. There are no prophets among the laity. A prophet is a seer. He has visions and revelations and can interpret the plan of God for the Church. He points the way and speaks the mind of God for the moment. He speaks by sudden inspiration for the moment.

The Evangelist

The evangelist is a preacher. He preaches the good news of the gospel of the Lord Jesus Christ. He also has signs and wonders and miracles follow his ministry. This ministry has a drawing capacity because of the sign gifts and will draw people in from the north, south, east, and the west. Many are the conversions and miracles when the true office of an evangelist is seen.

The Pastor

The pastor has a shepherd's heart. He would rather leave the 99 sheep and go after the lost one. He has a love for the sheep and a desire to care for the flock of God. The pastor's grace to stand in that office is proportioned to the measure of the gift of Christ according to Ephesians 4:7.

The Teacher

The teacher is one who teaches not by natural ability, but by supernatural ability. He has the ability to stand before the flock of God and break the Word down and feed the flock. He has a strong desire to see them grow in the grace and knowledge of the Lord.

These Are Heavenly Gifts to the Church Given by Jesus

These fivefold ministry gifts cannot be imparted by man. We can only recognize the call and the anointing on an individual's life. There are no fivefold callings among the laity.

Some of the places where I go people tell me, "Brother Rodney, I am a part-time prophet." If you are part time, obviously the gift that is on your life can't be worth much. The Bible says that a man's gift shall make room for him (Proverbs 18:16). If he is part time, then he couldn't have much of an anointing on his life. Otherwise, he would be full time in the ministry. God pays for what He orders and where He leads, He feeds, and where He guides, He provides.

The Misuse of a Position of Authority

We must realize that just because an individual is called as an apostle or prophet does not give that individual the right to lord it over the whole Body of Christ. You are only an apostle to whom you are sent, not everyone in the church. Some try to lord it over the whole Body of Christ and operate in almost a cult-like manner when they demand respect and take the authority where it's not due them. Authority comes from the anointing; respect only comes by the anointing.

The only way some cults or even some Pentecostal and charismatic churches exist is not through godly leadership with anointing, resulting in respect, but through intimidation and fear. The leaders are saying, "If you leave this church you are going to hell. If you don't tithe you are going to hell. Don't even question my authority." They manipulate and control and humiliate and intimidate people to the point where some think that if the minister rejected them, then God was rejecting them.

God does not give the ministry gifts to manipulate and control the church, but rather to lead and serve the church. Remember, the last thing Jesus ever did before He went to the cross was He washed the disciples' feet. We must be a servant to all, but a slave to none.

Accountability to the Word

I am not leader bashing, but I feel there must be an accountability to the Word of God. We must realize that God does not give ministers the right to usurp their authority and brutalize the sheep. Jesus is the chief shepherd and we are accountable to Him.

No wonder the scripture says that those who will be teachers will receive the greater condemnation (James 3:1). I think recent events in the Body of Christ have proven that any leader, however great he might be, can come down.

Every Man Will Be Brought Low

I remember I was in a meeting with several thousand people and we were worshiping God and two great men of God walked onto the platform. The people quit worshiping God and began to whistle and shout. Immediately, I began to weep and apologized to the Lord saying, "I am so sorry that we stopped worshiping You and began to worship these men." The Lord said to me, "Every man will be brought low, but Jesus will be lifted up."

It is so important that we realize we cannot and must not touch the glory. If anyone does, it will lead to their downfall. There are those who even at this time

teeter on the brink of destruction and unless God super-
naturally intervenes, they will surely fall.

Some Are Called, Some Are Sent, Others Bought a Microphone and Went

The ministry is not a job or a vocation. It is not
something you decide to do for a living. It's a call, a
supernatural, divine call. The scripture says, "Many be
called, but few chosen" (Matthew 20:16). The scripture
says, "Ye have not chosen me, but I have chosen you"
(John 15:16).

Some people think that if you can't be successful in
business then you need to go into the ministry or if you
are successful in business then you will make it in the
ministry. It's neither. It has to do with the call of God.

The Ministry is Spelled W-O-R-K

Others think that God will reward laziness in the
ministry, but I want you to know that Jesus didn't go
walking through the park and find Peter the tramp,
James the Hobo, and John the Bum and say, "Follow Me,
I'll make you fishers of men." They were busy working
as fishermen, then He came and called them.

I like what Charles Finney used to say. "I get down
and pray like it all depends on God, and then get up and
go like it all depends on me." The ministry is not for
lazy people but for people who are working for the Lord
with all their might. The Bible says, "I must work the
works of him that sent me, while it is day: the night
cometh, when no man can work" (John 4:9).

The Call of God

The call of God is a holy call. It is something
beyond the ordinary. It is something that you will never
get away from. It will be something that will burn in

your life and literally consume you. There should be no unused members in the Body of Christ.

Problems have arisen because people just sit like a bump on a log, waiting to get a platform somewhere, waiting for Brother or Pastor or Doctor Whoever to give them a platform and let them preach. Your platform starts at home, your platform starts on the sidewalk, your platform starts in the street.

Despise Not the Day of Small Beginnings

I remember when I started in the ministry. Nobody wanted me. If I called a pastor and said, "We are passing through town...," they said, "That's wonderful, just keep passing through."

Even though at that time nobody wanted me, I knew that God had called me to preach. He had anointed me in 1979 and I hit the ground running. I would preach anywhere the opportunity arose. It didn't matter if there were two people. It didn't matter who was there.

I would go and find an auditorium in a small city somewhere, only seating a couple of hundred people. I had thousands of handbills printed up and advertised a four-day crusade. I walked out the first night and saw there were eight people sitting there. I rejoiced. I had eight more people than what I had before I started. I went out and preached up a storm.

Then after three nights, we ended up with forty people and I thought I had a Holy Ghost revival. Ten people got saved, three people got baptized in the Holy Ghost, two deaf ears were opened. I can look back on that now and rejoice because I can see where we have come from.

You Need Something That You Can Fall Back On

People would come to us in the early days and I realize now that they were trying to help. They would say to me, "You know, maybe you need to sell insurance on the side. Maybe you can sell gold coins or air purifiers or something that everyone needs and sell it on the road. It will at least be something to fall back on if the ministry does not work out."

I would be indignant and refuse and then they would say to me, "Well, maybe your wife could sell something on the side to help sustain you in the ministry. You need something to fall back on."

I would look at them and what they would say would really irritate me. I would get mad and say, "Bless God, He called me to preach and I am going to preach and I don't care what anybody says. I will not quit. I am going to preach the gospel. I don't care if it tears up the whole nation, but I am going to preach the gospel from one nation to the other. We are going to do what God has called us to do." Every year I would tell my wife, "Honey, next year has got to be better than this one; it can't be worse."

When you begin in the ministry, there are hard times, but you have to purpose in your heart that you will not quit. There is no turning around. I would rather die than to stop doing what God has called me to do. I will not quit doing what the Spirit of God has called me to do.

Paying the Price

Over a period of time, you start to find your niche. You start to find your purpose, you start to find the plan, you start to find the direction, you start to learn which way God is taking you. It is not something that happens overnight. The Bible says, "Many be called, but few chosen" (Matthew 20:16). I could even term it this way, "Many are called and some are frozen."

God has called people and anointed people, but a lot of them will never fulfill the call of God on their life because they are not prepared to pay the price. They are not prepared to do what God has called them to do. Or they are not prepared to be faithful in the little. If you are not going to be faithful in the little, God cannot make you a ruler over much.

I believe God will use the whole Body of Christ in this last day and I believe there are people in churches right now who have been sitting there for ten, fifteen, twenty years, receiving the Word, who in these last days will have an encounter with God. They will have a visitation from the Lord and God will send them in a matter of two or three months. They will sell all their possessions and go on to a foreign field and serve the Lord Jesus Christ. I believe that with all my heart. So never say, "God couldn't use me."

Everyone is called to stand in the ministry of reconciliation, one on one, to tell others, to proclaim. Everyone should be a preacher — a proclaimer — of the blessing of the Lord Jesus Christ. You can start in your workplace. If you are faithful with that, God might just increase it and get you into some other places.

Don't Go Without a Message

When I lived in South Africa, I was teaching at a Bible school that had about four hundred students. I had to teach them twice a day, five days a week, on different subjects. I would say to them, "How many of you are going to preach?" Everyone raised their hand. I said, "How many of you have a message," and no one responded. "How many would like a place to preach?" Everyone raise their hand. Then I said to them, "Get a message from God first, and then get a place to preach."

What is good in having places to preach if you don't have a message when you get there? Do you know how many ministers are that way? They look for places to preach and when they get there they haven't got a message to give. God will give you a message. God will give you a word and when you are faithful to deliver that, He might give you some more.

Such As I Have

As the Apostle Peter said, "Silver and gold have I none; but such as I have give I thee: In the name of Jesus Christ of Nazareth rise up and walk" (Acts 3:6). We must give what we have on the inside of us. It flows forth out of us, bringing life wherever we go. People look at my ministry today after thirteen years and say, "It is so wonderful how things are going and God is blessing." But they don't know we have been to hell and back to get here.

We must have the determination to obey God and to keep doing what God has called us to do. We cannot worry about what other people say, or the rejection that will come our way. We cannot be hindered by people who will talk evil about us, who will make up stories about us, who will slander us.

You make the decision in your heart to walk in love and to obey God and do what God has called you to do. Ultimately, when it comes down to the bottom line, it's you and God. No one else is going to make it happen for you. If you are waiting for some hand out, you can forget about it.

Start doing whatever your hand finds to do. There is a progression into the things of God, into the anointing. These things don't come overnight. God is not going to take a ministry, like some of the great men of God have had, and suddenly give it to you in one day. It takes time.

Prepare and Press In

It is interesting to note that Jesus spent thirty years of His life preparing for three and a half years of ministry. Today people go to Bible seminaries and prepare three years for thirty years of ministry. There must come preparation.

You are always in continuous preparation for the next phase of what God has for your life. I know in my own life that even after the encounter I had with the Lord in July of 1979 until the present, I am still in preparation for what God has for my life and ministry. I am not satisfied with what we are doing and I know that there is more that is available. I want to push higher and deeper into the things of God.

Smith Wigglesworth said that the only thing that he was satisfied about was the fact that he was dissatisfied. We don't ever want to get to the place of lethargy and complacency, satisfied with where we are. Otherwise we will never press in to what God has for our life and ministry.

Dissatisfaction with where you are now will cause you to arise and press in to what God has told you to do. It is time to get off your blessed assurance and start acting upon the Word of God. Start doing whatever your hands find to do and then the anointing will increase.

Chapter 5
Different Kinds of Anointings

We see that in the Word of God there are different kinds or types of anointings given to man. Ephesians 4:7 says, "But unto every one of us is given grace according to the measure of the gift of Christ." The word grace means enablement, ability, or anointing. We have already seen in chapter one that the anointing is the supernatural equipment to get the job done.

In Luke 4:18, 19 Jesus said, "The Spirit of the Lord is upon me, because he hath anointed me to preach the gospel to the poor; he hath sent me to heal the broken-hearted, to preach deliverance to the captives, and recovering of sight to the blind, to set at liberty them that are bruised, To preach the acceptable year of the Lord."

There Is an Anointing to Preach

Any preacher will tell you that the anointing to preach is like a fire shut up in your bones. You can't get rid of it. When the message burns deep in your heart, it has to come out and it does so with great power.

I think the greatest characteristic about preaching is the unction by which the message is delivered. Some think that shouting is preaching. Well, you might get excited and shout when God's power falls on you — I know that I do — but it really has to do with the unction to preach. God anoints your tongue and makes it as "the pen of a ready writer" (Psalm 45:1). You begin to speak as an oracle of God.

The scripture also says, "Is not my word like as a fire? saith the Lord; and like a hammer that breaketh the rock into pieces?" (Jeremiah 23:29). God's Word, when preached under an anointing, will bring conviction and bring a change in the lives of the hearers. Sermons are not meant to be enjoyed; they are meant to be adhered to.

Reprove, Rebuke, and Exhort

The Apostle Paul, in speaking to Timothy, said, "Preach the word; be instant in season, out of season; reprove, rebuke, exhort with all longsuffering and doctrine" (Second Timothy 4:2). I want you to notice he says, reprove — which means to admonish or to advise. Then he says, rebuke — which means to reprimand; and then, exhort — which means to encourage, to urge.

Two-thirds of preaching is reproving and rebuking and one-third is exhorting. One of the problems we have in the Church today is that many preachers would rather preach around an issue than address the issue. The Bible says in the last days, men would "heap to themselves teachers, having itching ears; And they shall turn away their ears from the truth, and shall be turned unto fables" (Second Timothy 4:3, 4).

The Art of Persuasion

If we study the ministry of Charles Grandison Finney, we find that he was not only criticized because of the manifestations in his meetings, but also because of his method of preaching. When he spoke about sinners, instead of saying, "they," he would say, "you." He would speak about hell in such a way that people would be shaken in their seats. In every message he forced a decision.

The art of preaching is not so much homiletics (three points and a poem), but rather the ability to bring people to the point of a decision. King Agrippa said to Paul, "Almost thou persuadest me to be a Christian" (Acts 26:28).

Charles Finney was a lawyer prior to entering the ministry. When he entered the ministry, he used his ability to take a subject and present it as a legal case. He would preach as though he were standing in front of a jury and needed to convince them. At the end, he would demand a decision from them.

This was his success in the ministry during an age when there was no radio, television, or amplifiers and microphones. He won about five hundred thousand people to Jesus. It is said of his converts that about 85 percent stayed true in their faith. In comparison to modern-day evangelism, we find this figure is extremely high.

There Is an Anointing to Teach

The teaching anointing is different from the preaching anointing. It is more subdued, but it has a definite flow to it. You will find that the teaching anointing carries revelation that causes the listener to see plainly and clearly what the Spirit of God is saying to the Church.

I am convinced in many circles today that instead of teaching the simple gospel of the Word of God, men are complicating the lives of God's people. Instead of teaching that brings one into freedom, they preach people into bondage and tradition.

Paul wrote to the Galatian church and said, "O foolish Galatians, who hath bewitched you?" (Galatians 3:1). You see, the Judaisers were preaching circumcision and trying to get the Galatian church back under the law. Paul said to them, "Having begun in the Spirit, are ye now made perfect by the flesh?" (Galatians 3:3).

Keep the Message Simple

We must keep the gospel simple to feed the flock of God, not choke them. Even Psalm 23:2 says, "He leadeth me beside the still waters." A true shepherd will not take his flock to drink in a fast-running brook. Because of the position of the sheep's nostrils, the sheep would drown. The shepherd cuts a U shape in the bank of the river and allows the water to run into it. The sheep can drink from the still water.

So it is in the church. Whenever the Word of God is taught with simplicity, then God's people will be set free and they will grow into maturity. There are some things that we can be dogmatic on such as basic Bible doctrines, the absolutes of God's Word. But we cannot and should not be dogmatic concerning the non-absolutes of God's Word.

In Africa, one of the animals that roams freely is the giraffe. The giraffe is known for its long neck. It has the ability to feed upon the leaves up high in the tall trees. The smaller animals, such as the little deer, cannot reach these tall trees and so have to eat on the ground.

Starving Sheep and Constipated Shepherds

Many ministers are feeding giraffes while the little deer are starving because they do not have the ability to reach the food. They do not even understand what is being preached.

I am disturbed by the fact that many people do not understand what is being preached from the pulpits of the land. They will sit in their pews and think, *I don't know what he's talking about.*

Then they observe others taking notes and they think to themselves, *Well, they understand what he's talking about. I know I don't, but then I have always been slow in understanding certain things.* But they should realize that the person taking notes didn't know what he was talking about either and was probably writing a note to a friend. If the truth were known, the preacher doesn't know what he's talking about himself.

Let's get back to the simplicity of preaching the gospel of the Lord Jesus Christ so that the sheep may be fed. You know, God's Word is so simple, you need an idiot to help you misunderstand it.

There Is an Anointing to Heal

We have to understand that there is an anointing to heal. The scripture says in Acts 10:38, "How God anointed Jesus of Nazareth with the Holy Ghost and power: who went about doing good, and healing all that were oppressed of the devil; for God was with him."

The anointing is the presence of God. We know that in His presence is the fullness of joy and so in His presence is healing divine. In His presence there is no lack.

Healing Through the Word

The healing anointing is manifested in several ways and we can see it in the scripture as healing through the Word. Psalm 107:20 says, "He sent his word, and healed them." Whenever the Word of God is spoken in faith from the lips of a believer, then God's healing power is activated. Jesus often spoke the word and many were healed.

Remember the story of the centurion who came to Jesus seeking healing for his servant? The centurion said to Him, "Speak the word only, and my servant shall be healed. For I am a man under authority, having soldiers under me: and I say to this man, Go, and he goeth; and to another, Come, and he cometh; and to my servant, Do this, and he doeth it" (Matthew 8:8, 9). Jesus said that

He had not found so great faith in all of Israel. The centurion's servant was healed when Jesus spoke the word.

Healing Through the Gifts

We find that as God begins to use individuals in the operation of the gifts of the Spirit, they begin to function through that individual according to the proportion of his faith and according to his character.

First Corinthians 12:9, 10 speaks of the three power gifts of the Spirit. These gifts are given to the Church to do something. They are the supernatural gifts.

The gift of faith is a supernatural manifestation of God's faith imparted to man at a specific time, at a specific place, for a specific purpose. When that gift begins to operate, a great boldness comes in an individual's life. As supernatural faith is poured into your life, there is no room for doubt and unbelief. Those two terrible twins from hell leave when the gift of faith is in operation.

The gifts of healing is a supernatural gift of God's healing power for divers diseases without the use of doctors or medicine. When the gift is in operation, many are healed all over the place of divers diseases. Many times you will see the gifts of healing operating with the word of knowledge.

The gift of working of miracles is a supernatural intervention of God in the course of nature and it can be in the area of creative miracles. Acts 19:11, 12 says, "And God wrought special miracles by the hands of Paul: So that from his body were brought unto the sick handkerchiefs or aprons, and the diseases departed from them, and the evil spirits went out of them."

Healing Through the Laying on of Hands

Mark 16:17, 18 says, "These signs shall follow them that believe: In my name...they shall lay hands on the sick, and they shall recover." We will discuss this later in a chapter about the laying on of hands.

There is healing by the laying on of hands, but also healing through the Word because God's Word is anointed. The Word will heal when mixed with faith in the heart of the individual.

There is also healing through the gifts of the Spirit. We need to realize the healing anointing flows in different ways through different people.

God might use one minister in one way and then another in a different way. We must never put God into a box. God will not be dictated to by anyone. God is a God of variety, of diversity. I will discuss this in more detail in the chapter on the healing anointing.

You can minister by the laying on of hands, by a tangible anointing, or by faith in the Word of God and see healings take place. God does grace people with a special anointing to minister to the sick. One can also believe Mark 16 and lay hands on people in faith in the name of Jesus and see great things take place.

Different Callings Mean Different Anointings

I personally believe that the anointing is dependent upon the callings placed in the lives of ministers. We know that the scripture also says, "Stir up the gift of God, which is in thee by the putting on of my hands" (Second Timothy 1:6). One can either stir it up or let it lie dormant.

For example, the parable of the talents comes to mind as we think of the one man who was given one talent and another was given two talents and another five. The man with one talent buried his and ended up losing it.

As the saying goes, if you don't use it, you'll lose it. We must be faithful with that which God has given us.

If we are faithful with the little, God will make us a ruler over much.

Different Strokes for Different Folks

One ministry will emphasize healing, another preaching or teaching, another salvation, another the baptism of the Holy Spirit. It is because of this diversity that we need to recognize the whole Body of Christ and to understand that we need each other. The foot cannot say to the hand, "I have no need of you." And the eye cannot say to the ear, "I do not need you." If the whole body were an eye, where would the hearing be? (First Corinthians 12:15-17). We need one another.

Don't try to work out with your mind another man's anointing. If he is getting results and people are getting saved, healed, and set free, then glorify God for his wondrous works among men.

Look beyond the vessel and see the glory of God, for the scripture says we have this treasure in earthen vessels. In these last days, God is raising up a group of people who will flow together and stop criticizing one another and will accomplish great things for the Body of Christ.

It's All in the Anointing

There is a difference between the fivefold ministry and the laity, and the difference is the anointing. In our understanding of the anointing, we have to realize that it's God's grace upon man. In the book of Acts, the Bible says, "When they saw the boldness of Peter and John, and perceived that they were unlearned and ignorant men, they marvelled; and they took knowledge of them, that they had been with Jesus" (Acts 4:13).

God anoints us in our daily walk with Him. Every child of God has a ministry of reconciliation, but everyone is not called to the fivefold ministry. In Ephesians 4:7, the scripture says, "But unto every one of us is given grace according to the measure of the gift of Christ." You could say, "But unto every one of us is given ability, enablement, or anointing according to the measure of the gift."

Calling equals anointing and ability. God will not call you to do something without giving you the ability to get the job done. Those whom God calls, He anoints and appoints.

Chapter 6
How To Increase the Anointing

A Relationship and Not a Formula

There are several things that we can use to enhance the anointing in our lives. Let me say, at the outset of this chapter, the anointing is not a formula; it is a relationship.

Many are trying to imitate other great men of God. They want to walk their walk and talk their talk, but not out of a relationship with Jesus. They try to use it as a means to have God's anointing manifest in their lives. For example, some ministers hold a healing meeting so they can have a crowd, not so that they can get people healed. That's the wrong motive for wanting to see miracles take place.

I remember talking to individuals who wanted what Smith Wigglesworth had. They studied his life and found out that Smith Wigglesworth used to wake up at four o'clock in the morning and have communion. Then he would pray for three hours. So they began to do the same. But after a little while, they would wake up late in the morning, realizing that they had fallen asleep, instead of praying.

This action was based on a formula and not a relationship. It is important to realize that Smith Wigglesworth did not do all of those things in order to have miracles in his life. He had a relationship with the Lord, and then out of his relationship, he ministered and the miracles were the result.

The Bible says, "When they saw the boldness of Peter and John, and perceived that they were unlearned and ignorant men, they marvelled; and they took knowledge of them, that they had been with Jesus" (Acts 4:13). Can people tell that you have been with Jesus lately? What Peter and John had was not based on a formula, but rather a relationship with the Lord Jesus Christ.

A Person, Not a Language

I think one of the biggest problems in many Pentecostal and charismatic circles is that people seek a language and not the Holy Spirit. First of all, the Holy Spirit is not a language; He's a person. Jesus said to the disciples, "Tarry ye in the city of Jerusalem, until ye be endued with power from on high" (Luke 24:59).

Some people think He said, "You will receive tongues." What good is tongues without the power? We have many babbling believers today with very little power.

When He told them to tarry for the Holy Spirit, they didn't know what they were waiting for. If there had come a knock on the door and someone walked in and said, "I am the Holy Spirit," I am sure they would have welcomed that person and said, "Yes, Jesus said You were coming."

But on the day of Pentecost, there came a sound from heaven as of a rushing, mighty wind. There appeared unto them cloven tongues as of fire and it sat upon each of them. They were all filled with the Spirit and began to speak with other tongues. (See Acts 2:1-4.)

I want you to notice they were filled, then they spoke. They were filled first. Power was evident in their lives. You see, the early church had the substance and unfortunately, the latter church has the formula. Let's get back to the substance, the tangibility, the heavenly materiality of what the early church had.

Having an Encounter with God

I believe if we would be used of God, we need to have an encounter with Him. Paul talked about how he had seen the Lord in the way. Moses had a burning bush experience. To be honest with you, so did everyone who has ever been used of God.

Job had an encounter with God at the end of his ordeal. God revealed Himself to Job, asking Job where he was when God laid the foundation of the earth. "Do you have a voice that can thunder like me?" God asked Job (Job 40:9).

Job finally spoke to God. His words speak for many people, I think. He said, "I have heard of thee by the hearing of the ear: but now my eye seeth thee" (Job 42:5). It's one thing to read the book; it's another thing to meet the author of the book.

The Life of Prayer

First of all, what is prayer? Prayer is communication and it's two ways. In many believers' lives, prayer is a one-sided conversation. They pray, "Give me, give me." They are always asking.

Prayer for the believer should not be a religious ritual performed on a daily basis by a Christian who wants to attain a certain level of spirituality. It should be a daily fellowship with our heavenly Father out of love.

We have to realize that we are not under the Old Covenant, but under the New. Whatever is done under the New Covenant must be done out of faith and love. Otherwise, it is nothing more than dead works, something that needs to be repented of.

A Lifestyle of Prayer

Every believer needs to develop a lifestyle of prayer. The Word says, "Pray without ceasing" (First Thessalonians 5:17). We need to realize that we can live in the spirit of prayer, whereby we pray all the time. Our heart can always be crying out to Him. Our thought life is never far away from God.

I asked the Lord why some people never feel or sense His touch in their lives. It's because most of their waking moments are caught up in the affairs of this life. Their hearts are far from God.

Jude 20 says, "But ye, beloved, building up yourselves on your most holy faith, praying in the Holy Ghost." It is important to pray in the Spirit and keep yourself built up spiritually. Some would say, "I need to get prayed up." Don't just get prayed up; stay prayed up. Stay in the Spirit.

Different Rules for Different Prayers

We know that just as different sports have different rules, so there are different kinds of prayer and not all prayer has the same rules. For the believer who would be used of God, there are two prayers especially among all the others that need to be prayed.

The first is the prayer of consecration. Jesus prayed this prayer in the Garden of Gethsemane. It was a prayer of consecrating His will to do the will of His Father.

The second prayer is the prayer of repentance, always keeping our hearts right with God. This is not on the basis of sin consciousness, but out of our love for Jesus. We would not want to do anything to hurt Him in any way, shape, or fashion.

These two prayers are lacking in many lives. For those who desire to have the anointing, a consecrated, yielded, repentant heart will be used of God.

Is God a Captive in His Own Heavens?

There are those in the Church who think that to see revival our prayer life must be directed towards the devil in a warfare attitude. They believe we must wage war on the devil in the heavens to release God so that He can move freely. They act as if God is bound in the heavenly realm, waiting desperately for a believer to loose Him so that the plan and purpose of God can be done on earth.

Honey, I Blew up the Devil and other Nintendo Games

This game of spiritual warfare is nothing more than a spiritual nintendo game played by baby Christians who have no understanding that Jesus defeated the devil two thousand years ago. He has sent the Holy Ghost to empower the believer and to flow through that individual's life to enforce the devil's defeat.

In this game, the devil is seen through the eyes of the believer as very big and in control. God is having a problem containing him. Believers, instead of preaching the gospel, are in their closets waging war on the devil. Many live in a fantasy world of spiritual warfare. It's probably the result of a bad dream and an overdose of pizza with too much cheese.

This has permeated the Church, infiltrated the worship, prayer, and study of the Word to such an extent that when you go to some churches, you wonder who are you going to worship. All they ever seem to do is talk about the devil and pray about what he is doing.

sermon and even their heavenly language is directed towards the devil.

By the end of the service, all the believers are stamping their feet, binding and loosing in a frightened frenzy. It reminds me of a bunch of kids who have been told they are going to have to walk home in the dark past a graveyard after they've just seen a horror movie.

Pulling Down Strongholds in the Mind or Heavenlies?

(For the weapons of our warfare are not carnal, but mighty through God, to the pulling down of strong holds;) Casting down imaginations, and every high thing that exalteth itself against the knowledge of God, and bringing into captivity every thought to the obedience of Christ (Second Corinthians 10:4, 5). This speaks of a warfare in the mind of man rather than in the heavenlies.

We have no account of Paul or anyone else — including Jesus — indulging in these so-called warfare practices. This practice is based on Daniel's 21-day fast while the angel was trying to get through. This, of course, is Old Covenant. The Holy Ghost is here on earth now. He came on the day of Pentecost and never left.

So rather than indulging in religious practices that do not produce any fruit, let us turn to the proclamation of the gospel linked to the demonstration of the power of the Holy Ghost resulting in the establishment of the kingdom of God. "The kingdom is not meat and drink; but righteousness, and peace, and joy in the Holy Ghost" (Romans 14:17).

It is interesting to note that the greatest soul winners in the world have never indulged in such practices. They have spent their time in prayer, fellowshiping with the Lord on a daily basis, and ministering out of an overflow of that communion with Him.

What Did Jesus Do?

When Jesus was tempted of the devil, He did not cast him down, but said, "It is written." When He stood at the tomb of Lazarus and prayed, it was not out of desperation, but for the benefit of those around Him. He turned first toward heaven, speaking only to God, not addressing demonic realms. Then out of His relationship with His heavenly Father, He proclaimed the desired result. (See John 11:41-44.)

Also, in the country of the Gadarenes, the demons knew who Jesus was. They said, "Have you come to torment us before our time?" They knew that their time was not yet and they pleaded with Him to cast them into the swine. He did, not in a three-hour battle, but with one word — go! (See Mark 5:1-14.)

There Is a True Intercession

I am not against true intercession which is the Holy Ghost praying through us the perfect will of God for any situation. But I am against fleshly prayer that produces nothing but pride in the individual's life and robs them of their joy and peace and their productivity in the kingdom of God.

A city like Los Angeles, California, is a classic example of a city that in recent times has been bombarded by prayer in some form or another. Yet it has seen anything but revival. It has seen earthquakes, racial rioting, drought, and more. I am not saying that we will not see revival come to L.A. If and when it comes, it will not be to the credit or glory of men, but through the outward working of the Spirit of God through men, resulting in many won into the kingdom of God.

Fact or Fiction?

Again, I must emphasize that I am not against true intercession. But remember that the devil realizes he can't stop the Church from prayer. He can, however, get us praying in the wrong direction. This will result in nothing but dead works, frustrating the believer and causing him to be caught up in a superspiritual world of warfare and demonic forces, fighting a seemingly never-ending battle. Yet he is never doing the works of Jesus — preaching, teaching, and demonstrating the power of God.

And even if he or she did minister, it would not be with an overcomer's mentality of seeing the victory purchased at Calvary as a finished work. Instead it is a warfare mentality seen through the eyes of a Christian writer's novel. The truth is, Jesus has already won the war and given us power and authority.

The Red Rag Mentality

The Church reminds us of a bull in a ring chasing a red rag as his opponent, not realizing it is the matador holding the rag who is his problem. If the bull ever found out the truth, that would be the end of the matador. Even so, the Word of God declares that when the enemy is revealed on that day, many will be amazed. They will say, "Is this the one who did bring kings down?" Many, including the Church, will be astounded.

We need to realize that the devil is defeated. He is not omnipresent and he is a creation, not creator. These simple truths will help us to see clearly that prayer must be used primarily to fellowship with the Lord and to spend time being filled up in His presence. Then out of an overflow of His touch, we minister to the needs of hurting humanity.

The Study of the Word of God

Paul, in speaking to Timothy, said, "Study to shew thyself approved unto God, a workman that needeth not to be ashamed, rightly dividing the word of truth" (Second Timothy 2:15). Every believer needs to have a workable knowledge of God's Word. One of the problems we face is that many Christians don't even know the basics of the Word. They are caught up in the non-absolutes of the Word. It is not producing life and joy and freedom, but rather death and bondage to man-made doctrines and forms.

The scripture says many walk after the doctrines of men, "having a form of godliness, but denying the power thereof" (Second Timothy 3:5). That is why Paul admonished Timothy to, "Preach the word; be instant in season, out of season; reprove, rebuke, exhort with all longsuffering and doctrine. For the time will come when they will not endure sound doctrine; but after their own lusts shall they heap to themselves teachers, having itching ears" (Second Timothy 4:2, 3).

Don't Throw Arrows in the Dark

The study of the scripture should be systematic, rightly dividing between the Old and the New and between absolutes and non-absolutes. It is evident that many take a little of the Old and a little of the New and make up their own covenant. It is one that brings them into freedom for a little while and then puts them back into bondage.

I suggest that once a believer has a workable knowledge of the scripture, then he or she spend time in the Epistles and also the Gospels. We should study the Epistles to find out what is available for us through the finished work of the cross. We should study the Gospels to follow closely the ministry of Jesus and to build into our lives an image of Jesus and His earthly ministry. Jesus said, "He that believeth on me, the works that I do shall he do also; and greater works than these shall he do" (John 14:12).

Any time spent in the Old Testament must be backed up with time spent in the New. Otherwise the student will come out with a picture of negativity and failure because the Old Testament was a type and shadow of the New. The Old without the New produces bondage and death.

The New Testament is the fulfillment of the Old and the completion of everything Jesus came for. That is why He cried, "It is finished," and the veil of the temple was rent in two from top to bottom. The Holy Spirit came out of an earthly tabernacle make with the hands of man, never again to live therein. He now lives in my heart and your heart. Thus the scripture says, "We have this treasure in earthen vessels" (Second Corinthians 4:7).

The Gospel Is Simple

If you do any study on issues, try not to get sidetracked away from the simplicity of the gospel. Do not run off on a tangent into something that does not produce life.

You will always know if you are into false doctrine when you begin to lose your joy and your peace. The scripture says, "In thy presence is fulness of joy; at thy right hand there are pleasures for evermore" (Psalm 16:11). Let peace be your umpire.

Allow the Holy Spirit to lead and guide you in your study of the scripture. Remember that the Holy Spirit is the teacher. He will take God's Word and make it alive for you. The letter kills, but the Spirit gives life.

Having a Hearing Ear

Jesus said, "My sheep hear my voice. The voice of a stranger they will not follow." (See John 10:5, 27.) It is interesting to find out that many Christians who have a "quiet time" really have a quiet time because they never hear from heaven. They never listen to see if God would actually speak to them.

"As many as are led by the Spirit of God, they are the sons of God" (Romans 8:14). God will lead you by His Spirit, but there needs to be a sensitivity to the anointing and it only comes with spending time in His presence. Only then do we recognize when God is speaking to us and instantly obey. In other words, we need to develop a hearing ear.

He That Has Ears to Hear

"He that has ears to hear what the Spirit is saying," is a phrase that is repeated throughout the New Testament. It's not talking about the natural ear, but the spiritual ear.

We know the story of Samuel and how he heard someone calling his name. He went to Eli and said, "You called me." Eli said, "I did not call you." This happened several times and then Eli realized that it was God who was speaking even though he did not hear that voice (not having ears to hear). He then said to Samuel, "Go lie down and when you hear the voice, say, 'Speak, Lord, for your servant is listening.'" (See First Samuel 3:1-10.)

The Case of the Broken Telephone

We have heard the sayings, "There is none so deaf as those who will not hear," and "People hear what they want to hear." I am reminded of a story I heard of a farmer who wanted God to speak to him. One morning, as he was sitting on his front porch of his farmhouse, a hand appeared and wrote in the sky the letters G P.

Instead of finding out any further information, the farmer sold his farm and went on the missionfield to fulfill his heavenly direction. After failing hopelessly and spending much time in prayer, he heard the Lord speak to him. He said, "What is the problem, son?"

The farmer said, "Lord, I obeyed You. I did what You told me. I read the letters in the sky and knew it meant, Go Preach." The Lord then said to him, "Son, the letters did not mean, Go Preach; they meant, Go Plow." In this man's zeal for God, he ran ahead and misinterpreted the will of God for his life.

Perfect Timing

It is interesting to realize that most people don't miss God in the general direction of what God has called them to do. Rather, they miss the timing, partly because they don't listen to what the Spirit of God is saying.

They have never developed their spiritual ear to the point of hearing God's voice more clearly. Instead, they are led by circumstances and situations in their lives. Blown by the winds of adversity, they wander around aimlessly, never accomplishing the will of God.

Charismatic Gurus, Have You Had Your Fortune Told Lately, and Other Horror Stories

Another scenario is that some Christians gravitate to so-called "prophets" — charismatic gurus of the day — to get another "word from God." But it's always something vague, something remote, and it never produces a workable, tangible reality in their lives.

After several years, the individual has a large collection of predictions, dating back over the years, and not one has come to pass. But it's another nail in the religious coffin of death and bondage.

The truth of the matter is that prophecy is confirmation, not information. The Bible says, "As many as are led by the Spirit of God, they are the sons of God." It does not say, "As many as are led by the prophets are the sons of God."

Following the Ministry of Jesus

I believe another way to increase the anointing is to spend much time reading the gospels and following closely the ministry of Jesus. Jesus said, "The Son can do nothing of himself, but what he seeth the Father do" (John 5:19). I believe we will only do what we see Jesus do.

The disciples followed Jesus and saw the signs and wonders and miracles that He did. He said to them, "He that believeth on me, the works that I do shall he do also; and greater works than these shall he do: because I go unto my Father" (John 14:12).

He sent the Holy Ghost to empower them that they might go forth and do His works. Later, when Peter and John were taken in front of the chief priests and elders and commanded not to preach or teach in the name of Jesus, they said, "We cannot but speak the things which we have seen and heard" (Acts 4:20).

You Will Be Like Those You Hang Around

You will only do what you have seen and heard. If you hang around a ministry that does not believe in healing and in the power of the Holy Spirit, then you will be just like that.

When people come to me and say, "I don't believe in miracles," or tell me that miracles have passed away, I tell them that they have come too late to convince me. I've seen God move. I believe in miracles.

Something that has been a blessing to me is reading about one of the miracles Jesus did. Then I close my eyes and watch what He did, picturing before my very eyes how exciting it would be to attend Jesus' crusades and to witness the miracles He did.

Looking For a Man; Missing Your Miracle

Let's look at the story of the man Jesus healed at the pool of Bethesda found in John 5:1-9. The Bible says there was by the sheep market a pool, in the Hebrew tongue called Bethesda, having five porches. In these porches lay a great multitude of blind, halt, and maimed people, waiting for the troubling of the water. At a certain season an angel would come and trouble the water and whoever stepped in first was made whole of whatever disease he had.

If you can, for a moment, picture the events that transpired. An angel would come down and trouble the water. Imagine how frustrating it must have been for those who had been waiting for years for their miracle. While they were coming, someone else got there ahead of them.

Jesus arrives on the scene and walks up to a man who was powerless to help himself. He asks him a question. "Wilt thou be made whole?" That seems a ridiculous question to ask a man who is sitting by a healing pool waiting for an angel to trouble the water. If he was from New York he might have said, "Of course, I want to be healed. What do you think I am sitting here for, my health?"

Jesus was provoking the man to see where he was. The man gave Jesus a ridiculous answer in response to the question. He said, "Sir, I have no man. While I am coming, another steps down and is healed in my place." Jesus didn't ask him if he had a man. He asked him,

"Wilt thou be made whole?" In reality, Jesus was saying, "I am your man. Rise, take up your bed, and walk." The man arose and walked.

Looking for the Missing Pieces of the Puzzle

Anyone reading this passage of scripture would say to me, "Well, Brother Rodney, isn't it wonderful that the man was healed?" Yes, it is wonderful. But when I read this scripture, something bothered me about this whole story and I couldn't put my finger on it.

I read and reread this passage of scripture and I could not help wondering, *If all those sick people were there, why did Jesus only heal one.* I could not understand why others around this man didn't shout out to Jesus and ask Him to come over and heal them as He had healed that man.

After praying about it, the answer suddenly dawned on me. It was so simple I could have kicked myself for not seeing it sooner. The reason the others were not healed was because they had a man to help them get into the pool. They were so busy looking to their man, they missed their miracle. Their miracle came into the midst of them, and then left. They were untouched because they were too busy to see what had happened right in front of them.

As we spend time in the Gospels and follow the ministry of Jesus, we begin to see it without the cloak of religion and in the power of the gospel.

Being Faithful to the Call of God

The anointing is not taught; it is caught. The only way to get the anointing is to be where the anointing is being poured out. Doing what God has called you to do will cause His power to flow through you.

One of the problems many ministers face is that they get discouraged when things don't go the way they would like. They end up quitting the ministry just prior to their breakthrough.

I believe the Lord is looking for those who will be faithful to obey the call. He will test you in the ministry before you see an increase. The scripture says if you are faithful over little, God will make you a ruler over much.

A Case of the Forgotten Son

The story of David is a wonderful story of a young man whom God had chosen to be king. God had spoken to the prophet Samuel and told him to anoint a king in Saul's place. Samuel went and stood in front of Jesse's sons and none of them was found eligible for the position of king. God had chosen David because of his faithfulness with a few sheep and the attitude of his heart. Even though he was out with the sheep, God knew where he was and anointed him in Saul's place.

David had been in preparation for the ministry. He was faithful to take the lion and the bear. Little did he know that God would have him take on a giant. Many even in the ministry today want the giant, but are not prepared or faithful to take the lion and the bear.

We live in a day and age of instant results. Many judge success by monetary gain or achievement of how many you have in your church, or how big your radio and television ministry is, or how big a mailing list you might have.

Success Is Doing What God Has Called You to Do

Success is doing what God has called you to do. I have had the privilege of being around some of the great men of God who pastor large churches. One of them publicly made the statement to other ministers that it didn't matter if you only had 100 people in your church.

If that was what God had called you to, then you should be content and happy in that ministry.

Privately I heard him make the statement about a pastor of a small church, "When he gets a thousand people in his church, then let him come and talk to me." In other words, he was saying the man was not worthy to talk to him because he was not in the same league.

I am reminded of a statement I used to tell the Bible students at a school in South Africa where I lectured several years ago. "Always remember the little man on your way up, because you might need him on your way down."

If the grace of God did not lead you to a certain place, then the grace of God cannot keep you there.

Legends in Their Own Mind

Another minister informed me — comparing his ministry to the ministry of another — that his ministry was a Cadillac and the other was a Yugo. I thought to myself, *Then I must be the hubcap on the Yugo.* One preacher informed a friend of mine that he was one of the top five speakers in the world today. I thought to myself, *I must be one of the bottom five.*

It is not what you have done or achieved in man's eyes that counts; it is faithfulness to the call of God. When I stand before my heavenly Father I desire to hear Him say, "Well done, thou good and faithful servant. Enter into the joy of the Lord." I don't want to hear, "Well done, thou good and successful servant You have already received your reward, it's the praise of men."

The Danger of Forgetting Where You've Come From

Is it not amazing that God visits an ordinary individual and anoints him? The man rises out of the dust to achieve greatness in God. Later when asked what was the key to his success, he gives a ten-point guideline to would-be followers about the secret to success.

But it had nothing to do with the ten points. It was the touch of God in the individual's life which resulted in the call. He remained faithful to fulfill the call and succeeded. It is as simple as that.

It Doesn't Come Overnight

Success does not come overnight; it is formed in the fires of life. In that crucible theories become proven and foundations are laid. Usually those who rise overnight, fall before daybreak.

Some look at the success that we've had in the evangelistic field in recent times in South Africa and the United States (and in comparison to others we have not even begun yet), and they will say to me, "Your ministry shot up overnight." All I can tell them is that it's been the longest night of my life.

The Importance of Worship

Jesus said, "The hour cometh, and now is, when the true worshippers shall worship the Father in Spirit and in truth: for the Father seeketh such to worship him" (John 4:23). Worship is so important, not just corporately, but also privately. As we begin to worship Him, the presence of the Lord will come upon us.

The scripture says in Psalm 91:1, "He that dwelleth in the secret place of the most High will abide under the shadow of the Almighty." Worship is that secret place. We need to develop a lifestyle of prayer. We need to develop a lifestyle of worship.

Integrity in Life and Ministry

It is very important to be oneself. We are living in a day and age when there is so much pressure to follow the crowd and be an echo instead of being a voice. I believe God wants to raise up voices in these last days. He wants those who will speak as an oracle of God.

There is a lack of integrity in the ministry today. I believe if we would be used of God on a continual basis, we need to develop character in the area of integrity.

We live in a day when men have very little integrity, not only in the world but also in the Church. The scripture says, "Who shall ascend into the hill of the Lord? or shall stand in his holy place? He that hath clean hands, and a pure heart" (Psalm 24:3, 4). It is sad to think that in the Church today there is a lack of integrity. People say what they want and then forget completely what they said. Some even deny that they said or promised anything.

The motto I have adopted in the ministry is, "Expect nothing from anyone, but commit yourself to be a giver." The Bible says God will honor a man who swears to his own hurt (Psalm 15:4). Many times when I am promised things from men of God, I don't get excited until I see it happen. It is sad that you cannot trust someone's word. The lack of integrity has plagued the ministry for many years, from the Elmer Gantry of Hollywood to real life, modern day televangelism.

Man Looks on the Outside; God Looks on the Heart

And the Lord said unto Samuel, How long wilt thou mourn for Saul, seeing I have rejected him from reigning over Israel? fill thine horn with oil, and go, I will send thee to Jesse the Bethlehemite: for I have provided me a king among his sons.

And Samuel said, How can I go? if Saul hear it, he will kill me. And the Lord said, Take an heifer with thee, and say, I am come to sacrifice to the Lord.

61

And call Jesse to the sacrifice, and I will shew thee what thou shalt do: and thou shalt anoint unto me him whom I name unto thee.

And Samuel did that which the Lord spake, and came to Bethlehem. And the elders of the town trembled at his coming, and said, Comest thou peaceably?

And he said, Peaceably: I am come to sacrifice unto the Lord: sanctify yourselves, and come with me to the sacrifice. And he sanctified Jesse and his sons, and called them to the sacrifice.

And it came to pass, when they were come, that he looked on Eliab, and said, Surely the Lord's anointed is before him.

But the Lord said unto Samuel, Look not on his countenance, or on the height of his stature; because I have refused him: for the Lord seeth not as man seeth; for man looketh on the outward appearance, but the Lord looketh on the heart.

Then Jesse called Abinadab, and made him pass before Samuel. And he said, Neither hath the Lord chosen this.

Then Jesse made Shammah to pass by. And he said, Neither hath the Lord chosen this.

Again, Jesse made seven of his sons to pass before Samuel. And Samuel said unto Jesse, The Lord hath not chosen these.

And Samuel said unto Jesse, Are here all thy children? And he said, There remaineth yet the youngest, and, behold, he keepeth the sheep. And Samuel said unto Jesse, Send and fetch him: for we will not sit down till he come hither.

And he sent, and brought him in. Now he was ruddy, and withal of a beautiful countenance, and goodly to look to. And the Lord said, Arise, anoint him: for this is he.

Then Samuel took the horn of oil, and anointed him in the midst of his brethren: and the Spirit of the Lord came upon David from that day forward. So Samuel rose up, and went to Ramah.

1 Samuel 16:1-13

God Takes the Foolish Things to Confound the Wise

I want you to see something about the anointing of God upon individuals. God doesn't choose whom we would choose. God doesn't look upon a person's qualifications. God doesn't look upon their education. God doesn't look upon their stature. Their abilities in the natural have absolutely nothing to do with Him placing His hand upon them.

For ye see your calling, brethren, how that not many wise men after the flesh, not many mighty, not many noble, are called:

But God hath chosen the foolish things of the world to confound the wise; and God hath chosen the weak things of the world to confound the things which are mighty;

And the base things of the world, and things which are despised, hath God chosen, yea, and things which are not, to bring to nought things that are:

That no flesh should glory in his presence.

1 Corinthians 1:26-29

A New Testament Example

But there was a certain man, called Simon, which beforetime in the same city used sorcery, and bewitched the people of Samaria, giving out that himself was some great one:

To whom they all gave heed, from the least to the greatest, saying, This man is the great power of God.

And to him they had regard, because that of long time he had bewitched them with sorceries.

But when they believed Philip preaching the things concerning the kingdom of God, and the name of Jesus Christ, they were baptized, both men and women.

Then Simon himself believed also: and when he was baptized, he continued with Philip, and wondered, beholding the miracles and signs which were done.

Now when the apostles which were at Jerusalem heard that Samaria had received the word of God, they sent unto them Peter and John:

Who, when they were come down, prayed for them, that they might receive the Holy Ghost:

(For as yet he was fallen upon none of them: only they were baptized in the name of the Lord Jesus.)

Then laid they their hands on them, and they received the Holy Ghost.

And when Simon saw that through laying on of the apostles' hands the Holy Ghost was given, he offered them money,

Saying, Give me also this power, that on whomsoever I lay hands, he may receive the Holy Ghost.

But Peter said unto him, Thy money perish with thee, because thou hast thought that the gift of God may be purchased with money.

Thou hast neither part nor lot in this matter: for thy heart is not right in the sight of God.

Repent therefore of this thy wickedness, and pray God, if perhaps the thought of thine heart may be forgiven thee.

For I perceive that thou art in the gall of bitterness, and in the bond of iniquity.

Then answered Simon, and said, Pray ye to the Lord for me, that none of these things which ye have spoken come upon me.

Acts 8:9-20

Character and the Fruit of the Spirit

Character is a subject that is not discussed in many circles today. Problems arise when ministries are growing too fast. In other words, the anointing upon the person's life has developed faster than the character of the individual. Ten or twenty years down the line, it blows up and the ministry comes to nothing because they didn't allow their character to develop.

They didn't walk in the fruit of the Spirit. They didn't walk in love. They didn't walk in the joy of the Lord. They didn't work on their marriage. They didn't make sure they had a solid foundation at home. They didn't take care of their children. Their children end up backsliding away from God. They end up in a divorce and things just don't have a solid foundation.

Counting the Cost

"No one builds a tower unless he counts the cost." Do you realize the cost of being involved in the ministry? It's glamorous to look like you are going into the ministry, but have you realized the cost? What price will you have to pay to walk in that place?

When I started in the ministry, I was, as they say in the military, gung-ho. I was ready for anything. If God wanted me to run an arctic expedition and preach to the Eskimos I would have done it. I was ready to go at the drop of a hat, without ever finding out what it entailed. Sometimes it is good to be that way, because if you knew what was coming up, you wouldn't go in the first place.

I am reminded when the Gulf War was on and the young men were going to the Persian Gulf. Different age groups were going. There were the eighteen-year-olds, just out of school, who had watched several Rambo movies. Then there were the guys who were twenty years older, who had been through the Vietnam War. They were going out of a different sense of duty.

The young man didn't know what he was getting himself into. The first time he dives in a fox hole and those mortars are flying over his head, he suddenly realizes he is in the middle of war. The older man knew what the commitment was because he had already faced the heat of the battle.

Coming Ready or Not

When you first enlist in God's army, you may not know what it entails. Sometimes you say, "Lord, I'm ready for this." That is the way I was. I would pray, "Lord, I'm ready for that. Lord, I'm ready to go here. Lord, I'm ready to do this."

The Lord said, "Rodney, sit down and shut up." I would get upset and complain, and the Lord said, "You are not ready."

Then you go through several years of saying, "I'm not ready, Lord, I'm not ready, I'm not ready." The Lord comes to you and says, "Now, Rodney, go and do that."

"O God, I'm not ready!"

He says, "Yes, you are."

You see, four or five years ago, you were ready in your own ability, but now you know you can't do it in your own ability. So you are ready in His ability. When we are not ready in our ability, when we feel the weakest, that is the time when the Spirit of God can rest the strongest upon us.

When I Am Weak Then I Am Strong

Like the Apostle Paul said, "When I am weak, then I am strong" (Second Corinthians 12:10). He was able to say this in the middle of trials and tribulations. Paul had a thorn in the flesh, which was not sickness and disease, but was persecution. Everywhere he went in his life and ministry, he was either shipwrecked, beaten, left for dead, spent time in jail, spent a night and a day in the deep — he always had troubles and persecutions.

Paul prayed, "Lord, remove this thing from me." Some people think he got rid of it. No, he didn't. The

Lord said to him, "No, I'm not going to remove it from you. My grace is sufficient for you. My anointing is sufficient for you. My ability is sufficient for you to bear this persecution."

So Paul said, "Most gladly therefore will I rather glory in my infirmities, that the power of Christ may rest upon me" (Second Corinthians 12:9). He didn't say anything about sickness. He said, "I will rejoice in my infirmities and my weaknesses that the power of Christ may rest upon me." Remember that the Lord sent Ananias to Saul to tell him the things he would suffer for the name of Jesus.

What Are You Made Of?

It is in that place of hardness, in the beginning of the ministry that you see what you are made of. A grape does not produce juice until it is squeezed. You cannot have grape juice and wine, until you squeeze the grape. Some people need to go through a little bit of pressure to produce. Sometimes they get into trouble because of their own stupidity. At other times, the hard place is where they develop character.

The Bible says God tested Abraham. Also in Jesus' ministry He was led by the Holy Ghost into the wilderness to be tempted of the devil. Some people don't understand how it is possible that the Holy Spirit will do that. But God wants to see what you are made of before He entrusts something great to you.

Nebuchadnezzar learned what the three Hebrew boys were made of when he put them in the burning, firey furnace. They found out what Daniel was made of when they put him in the lions' den.

You Have to Start at ABC to Get to XYZ

So many people want to start at point Z but they won't start at A. Until you are ready for ABC, you can't get to XYZ. Be faithful with the little God gives you. It might take five, ten, twenty, thirty or forty years to see it come to pass, but have the stickability.

Stay with what God has called you to do, irrespective of the rain, the sun, the snow, the winter, the summer, the spring, irrespective of adversity, trials, tribulations, and heartaches. Remain constant. Operate in the fruit of patience and continue in what God has called you to do. It will be a process, but God will move you into a place where the ministry will come forth and into maturity.

Kathryn Kuhlman went through hell and back before her great ministry was born. She experienced many failures and many hours of loneliness. She said that she knew the day and time when Kathryn Kuhlman died.

Many people think they are out there and no one recognizes them, but God knows and He sees. He looks upon the heart. He is looking for a yielded and a willing vessel.

There Is a Time to Come Forth

It is almost like a lady who becomes pregnant. She would love to have the baby immediately, because it will save her a lot of problems. We have had three children. I've been with my wife during every birth. So I know what my wife went through. It would have been much easier to have all three at one time. It would have taken nine months instead of twenty-seven.

As much as that lady wants to have her baby, she has to wait for the time for the baby to come forth. When a baby is born prematurely, it must be placed in an incubator in intensive care. In the case of extremely premature babies, their lungs are underdeveloped and the child has less chance of surviving.

It is the same with ministries. People have tried to give birth to a ministry prematurely and it doesn't last long. It will last a year, two years, or perhaps five years, and then fade away into nothingness.

Two Kinds of Ministries

There are two kinds of ministries in the earth today. There are the shooting star ministries that will come in a blaze of glory and disappear or blow up. Then there are the ministries that are solid, like the North Star. They will stand the storms of life. They will stand when everything else around is falling, when other ministries are quitting, when people are pulling out of the ministry, when the persecution gets hot. They will stand when they clamp down even more on the television preachers, when they mock the preachers in the newspapers and the media.

These are men of God who will say, "We are not going to compromise! We'll not back down on the healing ministry! We are not going to back down on casting out devils! We are going to arise and boldly proclaim the Word of God in Jesus' name! It doesn't matter if they end up locking us in jail. It doesn't matter if we go to a foreign field and we give our lives there. Let it be so. We will obey the call of God!" These are the kind of people God is looking for.

Chapter 7

My Testimony — When God First Anointed Me

When You Grow Up in the Fire, You Cannot Stand the Smell of Smoke

I was raised in a Pentecostal home and born again at the age of five. I later received the Holy Spirit into my life at the age of eight. As I was growing up, I continually saw supernatural manifestations in the church we attended. I also saw it in my home.

I remember on one occasion, my mother fell and broke her arm in three places. Her arm bone was jutted up above her wrist. My parents were sitting in the living room listening to a Kathryn Kuhlman tape back in the days of the reel to reel tape recorder.

After they had taken communion, our pastor came and laid hands upon my mom and the power of God went through her arm like pins and needles. She felt a burning fire running up and down her arm and she knew she was healed. Our pastor was a powerful man of God. Back in the fifties, he had gone into a deaf school and emptied it by the power of God. Every deaf person was healed.

When my mother said she was going to cut the plaster cast off because she was healed, I pleaded with her not to. I was only about six years old at the time. To me, if something was broken, it was broken. I thought if she took off the cast her arm would fall off!

She went into the bathroom and filled the tub with hot water and while she was cutting away the cast with a razor blade, she was praying in the Holy Ghost. A little while later, she came out of the bathroom totally healed by the power of God. This was only four days after she had broken her arm. It was a total miracle that astounded the medical profession — a proven, documented miracle.

What I am saying is that you cannot grow up seeing that happen without being affected as a child towards the reality of the power of the Holy Ghost.

The Family That Prays Together Stays Together

My parents would sometimes pray from seven in the evening until two in the morning. People would come to the house and not want to leave because the presence of God was there, the anointing of God was there.

We would sit at the table and my father would start to pray over the food. I could tell from the way he prayed whether we were about to eat or whether we would eat a little while later. The anointing of God would come upon him and he would begin to prophesy. My mother would put the food back into the oven. She knew we were about to have church!

Hungry and Thirsty for God

I knew that there was more, much more. During the years that would follow, I began to get hungry for God. In July of 1979, I cried out to God in sheer desperation. I wanted Him to manifest Himself to me and in me. I was hungry.

He told me that I had to hunger and thirst. At first I said to Him, "Why don't You just give it to me? I have served You all my life. I have been a good boy. I haven't done this, I haven't done that, as others have. God, I deserve it."

He said, "I'm not a respecter of persons. You come the same way everyone else does. You come in faith and you get hungry and you desire it. Then I'll give it to you."

You have to desire it like a man who has been in the desert three days desires water. All he can cry for is water. If a man walks up to him and offers him half a million dollars, he will push him aside and shout, 'No, water, water, water!' He wants water more than life itself, because the only thing that is going to save him is water.

When you become desperate for the Holy Ghost in your life like that, so that you want nothing else, then He will come. There is something about a hungry and thirsty heart that will cause God's power to move over a million people and come to your house.

Baptism of Fire

As I prayed that day, I told the Lord, "Either You come down here and touch me, or I am going to come up there and touch You." I was desperate. I must have called out to God for about twenty minutes that day.

73

Suddenly the fire of God fell on me. It started on my head and went right down to my feet. His power burned in my body and stayed like that for three whole days. I thought I was going to die. I thought He was going to kill me. I thought, *He has heard my prayer, "Either You come down here and touch me or I will come up there and touch You," and now He has come down here and touched me and He is going to kill me and take me home.*

I was really praying, "Lord, I am too young to die." In the forth day, I am not praying, "O Lord, send your glory," I am praying, "Please lift it off me so that I can bear it." I was plugged into heaven's electric light supply and since then my desire has been to go and plug other people in.

My whole body was on fire from the top of my head to the soles of my feet. Out of my belly began to flow a river of living water. I began to laugh uncontrollably and then I began to weep and then speak with other tongues.

Drunk on the New Wine

I was so intoxicated on the wine of the Holy Ghost that I was literally beside myself. The fire of God was coursing through my whole being and it didn't quit. I began to realize why we would need a glorified body when we get to heaven. When the natural comes in contact with the supernatural, something has to give way and it's not going to be the supernatural.

He did finally lift that intense anointing off me, but it stayed lightly on me, that I was aware of, for two weeks. Because of that encounter with the Lord, my life was radically changed from that day on.

Chapter 8
How To Release and Transfer the Anointing

It is one thing to be anointed of God. It is another thing to be in a position to release that anointing to others, seeing their lives touched with the reality of that heavenly materiality.

After the encounter I had with the Lord in July of 1979, I made plans to go into the full-time ministry. In January of 1980, at the age of eighteen, I joined a group that traveled our nation, ministering in Word and music in many of the nominal mainline denominations across our country.

The group that I joined was interdenominational, but non-charismatic in their beliefs. They frowned upon the Pentecostal experience, but I felt led of the Lord to work with the vehicle they were providing me to spread the gospel. I knew that at anytime I could have been given the left foot of fellowship because I held fast to my Pentecostal experience.

The Day My Ministry Changed

I can remember the day it first happened — the day my life and ministry was to change. It was a day like every other. The interesting thing was that I was not doing anything that you might think I should have

75

been doing to bring this on. I believe it was all in the plan of God.

We were preaching in a Methodist church. I was back in the vestibule — which is a holy name for a plain, old office — preparing for the service. One of the young ladies came into the office and asked me to pray for her because she was in terrible pain. I stood up from the chair where I was sitting and lifted my right hand as I normally would do to lay hands upon her and pray. Then the most amazing thing happened.

Hey, This One's Loaded!

I got my hand halfway to her head, almost like a gunslinger would draw a gun out of a holster and point it at his opponent. Suddenly, unexpectedly, it felt like my finger tips came off. I felt a full volume of the anointing flow out of my hand. The only way I can explain it is to liken it to a fireman holding a fire hose with a full volume of water flowing out of it. The anointing went right into her. It looked like someone had hit her in the head with an invisible baseball bat and she fell to the floor.

I was left standing there totally dumbstruck by what had happened, looking at my hand and at the young lady. I was still conscious of the presence of God flowing out of me, but I was amazed at what had just transpired. About that time, the rest of the team walked in the door. I prayed for them and they all fell out under the power of God.

After a while, I managed to sober them up. I was afraid the priest would walk in the door and I would have some explaining to do. We then moved into the sanctuary and the service began. I was so overwhelmed by the experience and what I had witnessed that I couldn't get it out of my mind.

Call All Those Who Want a Blessing

I began to talk to the Lord all the while I was speaking in the service. I was asking Him what we (notice I said we) were going to do about what had happened. After all, I was not allowed to talk about the Holy Spirit, speaking in tongues, or falling under the power. But they didn't realize when you talk about Jesus, the Holy Spirit comes along to find out who you are speaking about.

Here I am, having a conversation with the Lord, asking Him what are we going to do. Suddenly He says to me, "Call all those who want a blessing."

Now, I was in a Methodist church, and if you asked a question like that, the whole church would respond. And respond they did. Let us keep in mind that I had said nothing about the Holy Spirit, speaking in tongues, or falling under the power.

They came and stood in one line across the front of the church. The Lord then said to me, "Don't lay both of your hands upon them." We have a problem with folks who are under the impression that ministers are pushing people over. The Lord said to me, "Just lay one finger of your right hand on the forehead of each individual and say, `In the name of Jesus.'"

I walked over to the first person and said, "In the name of Je..." I did not even have time to say, "sus," when the power of God threw that person to the floor. I went down the line and everyone went out under the power. They hit the floor just like someone had slammed them in the head with a Louisville Slugger.

This Is That

Many of them, the moment they hit the floor, began to speak with other tongues as the Spirit gave utterance. Others were pinned to the floor for up to one and a half hours. I turned and looked at the priest and said anxiously, "It wasn't me. It wasn't me."

As people began to get off the floor, they would come to me and ask the question, "What is this?" I answered them and said, "This is that." They then said, "This is what?" I quoted Acts 2:16-17, "This is that which was spoken by the prophet Joel; And it shall come to pass in the last days, saith God, I will pour out of my Spirit upon all flesh." They remarked, "Oh, is that what it is?"

This experience, to say the least, totally overwhelmed me. The anointing that I had tangibly felt stayed on me, manifesting in that way for about two weeks and then it subsided. It did not leave altogether, but did not manifest in the same way anymore.

This disturbed me. I began to pray and ask the Lord what I could do to get that anointing in full manifestation again in my life. I must be honest with you. For a young man, just beginning in the ministry, this was a totally overwhelming experience. It was something that changed my life and the course of my ministry. It was something that I will never forget as long as I live.

I now began to want the anointing to manifest on people's lives just as I had witnessed it. I wanted to know from the Lord what I might do to have the anointing return in that fashion. I suppose I was looking for a formula — something I could do to get that anointing back in the way I had witnessed it.

It's All Me and Nothing to Do with You

The Lord then began to instruct me during times of prayer. The first thing He said to me was this: "Son, this anointing is all Me and has nothing to do with you." He said that it was as He wills, not as I will.

The Lord then said to me, "You are just a vessel through which I am flowing. You cannot earn this anointing; it's given as I will. If I gave you a key and you could get this anointing at anytime, you would begin to think it's all you and not Me. Because you know it is Me that is doing this, you will have to give Me all the glory."

Then I asked Him when I could see this anointing in my life. He told me, "This is a shadow of what is to come. Be faithful in that which I have called you to do. In the process of time, you will walk in it." He told me if He gave it to me now, I would be like a four-year-old with a shotgun. I would blow everything up, including myself.

After this, I continued my study along the lines of the anointing. I closely studied the Gospels and the book of Acts, looking at the ministry of Jesus and the apostles. Then I began to get in as many meetings as I could where mighty men of God were being used of the Lord. I would watch and learn.

The Scripture that Became a Reality to Me

A passage of scripture that has meant so very much to me on the subject of the transference of the anointing is Mark 5:25-34. It is a passage which I believe is the greatest scripture on the subject of the anointing in the entire Word of God.

And a certain woman, which had an issue of blood twelve years,

And had suffered many things of many physicians, and had spent all that she had, and was nothing bettered, but rather grew worse,

When she had heard of Jesus, came in the press behind, and touched his garment.

For she said, If I may touch but his clothes, I shall be whole.

And straightway the fountain of her blood was dried up; and she felt in her body that she was healed of that plague.

And Jesus, immediately knowing in himself that virtue had gone out of him, turned him about in the press, and said, Who touched my clothes?

And his disciples said unto him, Thou seest the multitude thronging thee, and sayest thou, Who touched me?

And he looked round about to see her that had done this thing.

But the woman fearing and trembling, knowing what was done in her, came and fell down before him, and told him all the truth.

And he said unto her, Daughter, thy faith hath made thee whole; go in peace, and be whole of thy plague.

Mark 5:25-34

The Touch of Faith

We see in this passage of scripture that this woman was in dire straits. She had spent all her money, going to doctors over a twelve-year period, and was not getting any better but was getting worse. Then she heard of Jesus. "She said, If I may touch but his clothes, I shall be made whole. And straightway the fountain of her blood was dried up; and she felt in her body she was healed of that plague" (Mark 5:28, 29).

Something interesting is that she was, first of all, illegal in touching Jesus. Under the law, anyone with an issue of blood found in a public place could be taken out and stoned. I guess she had weighed the consequences of being caught and decided that enough is enough. She had to touch the hem of His garment. You can almost see her saying to herself, "I will sneak my healing, and no one will know about it."

If we begin to look at Jesus, we see that He was on His way to Jairus' house. The Bible says that a multitude was thronging Him. If the Bible says, a multitude was thronging Him, it could have been anywhere from five to ten thousand people.

So one thing is certain. In a crowd such as this, Jesus must have been bumped or touched by the multitudes. Yet something happened when this woman touched the hem of His garment. Divine virtue or power, called "dunamis" in the Greek, flowed out of Jesus into her body and she was healed.

Placing a Demand on the Anointing

There were many others who must have touched Him that day as He was walking among the crowd. Yet this woman got healed. It was because she placed a demand on the anointing on the life and ministry of Jesus. I want you to know that dunamis, or virtue, flowed into the woman. She felt it flow into her and Jesus felt it flow out of Him. The anointing was tangible and it will always flow into an individual who places a demand upon it.

Her faith was in touching the hem of His garment. When she touched Him, she made the connection and was made whole. There are many other references to people touching Jesus and being healed. In the book of Acts, when the shadows of the apostles passed over the sick, they were healed.

Methods and Results

It is important to realize that the anointing flowing through different ministers might come through different methods. I get a little tired with preachers who criticize methods of the transfer of the anointing. For example, someone said to me that he didn't agree with an evangelist who blew on people. I said, "What's wrong with blowing on people?"

Jesus spat on people. He also breathed on them and said "Receive ye the Holy Ghost" (John 20:22). It's all a point of contact in which someone can release their faith.

There are many examples of this in the Bible from anointing oil in James 5:14, to anointed handkerchiefs and aprons in Acts 19:11, 12. Namaan dipped seven times in Jordan for his healing. After making clay with spittle, Jesus told a man to go and wash in the pool of Siloam. An angel was used to trouble the water at the pool of Bethesda. A brazen serpent was raised in the wilderness for healing. The Bible is full of examples of different, unusual methods used to get results.

One time Moses struck the rock, the other time he was supposed to speak to it. What about Saul trying to get David to wear his armor? David decided to go with his slingshot because it was proven. Too often, we think ours is the only method, but it isn't.

God Is a God of Diversity

Anyone that has been a student of church history will see that God uses ordinary people, but they have different methods. Thank God that we are not all the same. Thank God for diversity.

It makes me think of two mountain climbers, climbing the same mountain from two different sides, both convinced they are the only climbers on the mountain.

But you can imagine the shock when they both reach the summit at the same time.

Why should we argue over methods? Let's look at the fruit of the ministry. Jesus said, "Every tree is known by his own fruit" (Luke 6:44). In studying revivals of old, we find that God used different folks with different strokes to get the job done. The sooner we realize this, the sooner we will be able to see the touch of God in others' lives.

To Disagree Without Being Disagreeable Is Not Compromise; It's Maturity

I will be honest with you. There are ministers who I don't personally agree with. But I will tell you I know beyond a shadow of a doubt that the hand of the Lord is upon their lives. I rejoice that many lives are being touched by the power of God through their ministries. You have to be spiritually closed not to see that God is using them, even if you don't agree one hundred percent with their teachings or the way they look at things. If we can agree to disagree, we can all climb the mountain together.

Chapter 9
Do You Have Fresh or Stale Oil?

I was conducting a revival in a church when the pastor asked me if I would minister to the sick by the laying on of hands and anoint them with oil. I told him I would do it gladly and then I asked one of the ushers to bring me the anointing oil. He did, but before I even saw the bottle of oil, I smelled it. It stank. It was stale, rancid oil. I then sent the usher to get me some fresh oil — three-in-one Holy Ghost oil — down at the convenience store. I could not understand why people would want to use rancid, stale oil.

The Lord then spoke to me and said that was how many of His children smelled in the spirit. They stank from the stale oil of yesterday. What they have is old; it's stale. He desires His people to have something that is real, fresh, and vibrant.

Stop Living on Yesterday's Bread

God's plan for His people is to be anointed with fresh oil. Many Christians are living on yesterday's revelation, yesterday's bread. "I remember how it was back in 1919," they say. "I remember how it was back when I was growing up." "If only we could go back to yesteryear." "If only it were back during the healing revival." "If only it were back during the days of Brother Wigglesworth." "If only we could have walked in the days of Jesus and the apostles." Yet my Bible says, "Many prophets and kings have desired to see those things which ye see" (Luke 10:24).

A Church That Is Ready

You and I are living at the closing of the ages. We live at the most important time in human history. These exciting days are not the time to quit, not the time to throw up our hands in defeat. This is a time to work!

The Bible says we must work while it is still day because the night is coming when no man can work (John 9:4). Jesus is coming soon! He wants a Church that is ready; that is prepared. If we are going to reach the world we need to be filled with the Holy Ghost — filled with fresh oil.

It's the same as with an automobile. When you first purchase it, you have it serviced regularly and its oil changed so that it will last longer. If you would take so much care of something that is temporal, how much more should you take care of your heart and allow yourself to be serviced regularly be the Holy Spirit with fresh oil so your Christian life will be sustained by the excitement of serving God.

So many of God's people, instead of maintaining themselves, allow themselves to be bound by a religious spirit which robs them of their joy. No wonder some people backslide and grow cold in their Christian walk.

The Holy Spirit is Symbolized by Oil

One of the symbols of the Holy Spirit is oil. When you get oil, you stop squeaking. The Church has too many squeaky Christians — always complaining, always squeaking. If the service is too long — squeak! If they don't like the preacher — squeak! If the worship service is long — squeak!

When the Holy Ghost oil comes, then it will get rid of all the squeaks. Then you will run smoothly.

The Coming of the Bridegroom

But of that day and hour knoweth no man, no, not the angels of heaven, but my Father only.

But as the days of Noe were, so shall also the coming of the Son of man be.

For as in days that were before the flood they were eating and drinking, marrying and giving in marriage, until the day that Noe entered into the ark,

And knew not until the flood came, and took them all away; so shall also the coming of the Son of man be.

Then shall two be in the field; the one shall be taken, and the other left.

Two women shall be grinding at the mill; the one shall be taken, and the other left.

Watch therefore: for ye know not what hour your Lord doth come.

But know this, that if the goodman of the house had known in what watch the thief would come, he would have watched, and would not have suffered his house to be broken up.

Therefore be ye also ready: for in such an hour ads ye think not the Son of man cometh.

Matthew 24:36-44

Many Are Not Ready

In these last days there will be those who will say, "Where is the sign of His coming?" Let me tell you, He is coming! He wants you to be ready and the only way you are going to be ready is to be full of the oil of the Holy Ghost.

Who then is a faithful and wise servant, whom his lord hath made ruler over his household, to give them meat in due season?

> **Blessed is that servant, whom his lord when he cometh shall find so doing.**
>
> **Matthew 24:45, 46**

You should live as if Jesus is coming today — yet not expect Him for a hundred years. Be ready. There are too many people saying, "We can't send our children to college; Jesus is coming." "We can't get married now; Jesus is coming." "We can't buy a house now; Jesus is coming."

No, you should continue on and go about your daily life. Plan ahead, but be ready. He could come at any moment. Are you ready to die right now?

Ready for Anything

If you are not ready, you had better get ready. We have to stay ready. Be ready to preach, ready to pray, ready to give a testimony, and ready to die and face the Lord at any time.

> **Verily I say unto you, That he shall make him ruler over all his goods.**
>
> **But and if that evil servant shall say in his heart, My lord delayeth his coming;**
>
> **And shall begin to smite his fellow servants, and to eat and drink with the drunken;**
>
> **Matthew 24:47-49**

This is exactly what is happening to the Church right now. They are saying, "My Lord is delaying His coming." So they are smiting one another and eating and drinking with the world.

> **The lord of that servant shall come in a day when he looketh not for him, and in an hour that he is not aware of,**

And shall cut him asunder, and appoint him his portion with the hypocrites: there shall be weeping and gnashing of teeth.

Matthew 24:50, 51

An Empty Lamp at Midnight

Then shall the kingdom of heaven be likened unto ten virgins, which took their lamps, and went forth to meet the bridegroom.

And five of them were wise, and five were foolish.

They that were foolish took their lamps, and took no oil with them:

But the wise took oil in their vessels with their lamps.

While the bridegroom tarried, they all slumbered and slept.

And at midnight there was a cry made, Behold, the bridegroom cometh; go ye out to meet him.

Matthew 25:1-6

I am telling you, there is a cry in the Spirit that says, "Behold, the bridegroom cometh. Behold, the bridegroom cometh. Behold, the bridegroom cometh." He is coming! He is coming! It does not matter what you think. It does not matter what you believe or what your theology is. He is coming! He is not waiting for you to make up your mind and say, "Okay, Lord, You can come now." He is coming!

Then all those virgins arose, and trimmed their lamps.

And the foolish said unto the wise, Give us of your oil; for our lamps are gone out.

But the wise answered, saying, Not so; lest there be not enough for us and you: but go ye rather to them that sell, and buy for yourselves.

89

And while they went to buy, the bridegroom came; and they that were ready went in with him to the marriage: and the door was shut.

Afterward came also the other virgins, saying, Lord, Lord, open to us.

But he answered and said, Verily I say unto you, I know you not.

Watch therefore, for ye know neither the day nor the hour wherein the Son of man cometh.

Matthew 25:7-13

Do you want to be caught with your lamp empty? If you are not going for God, you are going against Him. If you are cold in your life and can't read your Bible, or you can't pray, or you can't worship God, then there is something wrong. You need the oil of the Holy Ghost to come into your life.

Prepare Your Heart

The time has come to get ready. God is speaking to the Church. The time of preparation is here. The time has come to lay aside every weight and every sin that so easily besets us (Hebrews 12:1). The time has come to prepare our hearts — to prepare the inner man — not our heads. It is time for God's people to have a breakthrough in the spirit. It is time for a breakthrough in the soul, a breakthrough in the body. The devil has kept the Church in bondage long enough.

When you get the oil of the Holy Ghost, it will come on you like a mighty fire. God will light a match of the fire of the Holy Ghost and will set you aflame. You will march through the land like a mighty firebrand, blazing the trail of the Holy Ghost.

If you will open your heart to the Lord Jesus Christ and hearken to the Spirit of God, He will send a flame forth right from where you are. It will burn through your city and your state. It will go into the foothills and plains. It will burn through the highways and byways. Revival will spread like a mighty fire and the glory of God will be seen!

A Fresh Outpouring

This is the day of the outpouring of the fresh oil of the Holy Ghost. It is for you and for whosoever will come and drink of the fountain of living water! Revival begins in you. Revival must begin in you! It cannot begin in your neighbor for you. Forget about everyone else. Concentrate on yourself. Where do you stand with God? How full is your lamp? How trimmed is your lamp? How ready are you? Forget about neighbors and family members. What about you?

> **Wherefore (as the Holy Ghost saith, To day if ye will hear his voice,**

> **Harden not your hearts, as in the provocation, in the day of temptation in the wilderness:**

> **When your fathers tempted me, proved me, and saw my works forty years.**

> **Wherefore I was grieved with that generation, and said, They do alway err in their heart; and they have not known my ways.**

> **So I sware in my wrath, They shall not enter into my rest.)**

> **Take heed, brethren, lest there be in any of you an evil heart of unbelief, in departing from the living God.**

> **But exhort one another daily, while it is called To day; lest any of you be hardened through the deceitfulness of sin.**

> **Hebrews 3:7-13**

A Hardened Heart

One of the problems in the Church is that it is hardened with the deceitfulness of sin. Daily we are to exhort one another. Don't ever say that you can make it without your brothers and sisters. Don't ever say you don't need to go to church. "We have tapes; we can listen to tapes," you say. "It is the only time we have to spend with the family."

The Bible says, "Not forsaking the assembling of ourselves together, as the manner of some is; but exhorting one another: and so much the more, as ye see the day approaching" (Hebrews 10:25). The day of Christ's return is approaching! We are closer today than we have ever been. There is an urgency in my spirit. The clock is ticking away and there is a job to be done.

> For we are made partakers of Christ, if we hold the beginning of our confidence stedfast unto the end;
>
> While it is said, To day if ye will hear his voice, harden not your hearts, as in the provocation.
>
> For some, when they had heard, did provoke: howbeit not all that came out of Egypt by Moses.
>
> But with whom was he grieved forty years? was it not with them that had sinned, whose carcases fell in the wilderness?
>
> And to whom sware he that they should not enter into his rest, but to them that believed not?
>
> So we see that they could not enter in because of unbelief.
>
> Hebrews 3:14-19

The Sin of Unbelief

You will not move in the Holy Ghost if you allow your heart to be hardened and if you allow it to be embalmed with unbelief. Some Christians believe nothing God is doing. If someone is raised from the dead, they ask, "How do you know he was dead?" If God blew the roof off they would say it wasn't bolted down properly. They are always skeptical, always full of doubt, always full of unbelief. We have to change! What is it that causes us to have unbelief? The deceitfulness of sin.

For the time is come that judgement must begin at the house of God.

1 Peter 4:17

Oh, people don't want to hear that! They want to stay with the "nice" scriptures. They attach all their faith to Philippians 4:19 and similar passages. Yet, First Peter 4:17 is just as much the Bible as Philippians 4:19.

The Bible says, "All scripture is given by inspiration of God , and is profitable for doctrine, for reproof, for correction, for instruction in righteousness: That the man of God may be perfect, throughly furnished unto all good works" (Second Timothy 3:16, 17). You must be thoroughly furnished. Let it be known to all men and to all the demons in hell that you are full of the oil of the Holy Ghost and that your lamp is trimmed.

Judgement Must Begin at the House of God

The time has come that judgement must begin at the house of God. "And if it first begins at us, what shall the end be of them that obey not the gospel of God? (First Peter 4:17).

Presently, the world is laughing. But they haven't seen God in His power and in His glory. They sit in their ivory towers and they mock the things of God and the move of God and the ministers of the gospel. The day is coming when God will say, "That's it! I've had enough." The power of God will sweep through the land. The glory of God will be seen. People will be mocking the Spirit of God and they will fall dead.

God is not mocked. God wants to purge the Church, to make it the vessel He wants. Then we will go forth in power and He will begin to judge the world. There will come some natural disasters too. Whole cities will be swallowed up in earthquakes. The Bible says, "In the last days, perilous times will come" (Second Timothy 3:1).

We Are on the Brink of the Greatest Move of God

We are living on the brink of the greatest revival of the Holy Ghost. Every one of you can be a part of it. If you will clean up your act and say, "God, I am so tired of everything. I don't desire anything but You. I just want to live for You. God, do whatever You have to do in my life. Change me, fill me with Your oil. I want to be a part of that move. I want to be in the ranks. I want to be part of Your army. I don't want to be left at boot-camp. I want to be out in the front lines!"

If the righteous scarcely be saved, where shall the ungodly and the sinner appear?

Wherefore let them that suffer according to the will of God commit the keeping of their souls to him in well doing, as unto a faithful Creator.

1 Peter 4:18, 19

God wants to do a work in your heart. But He is not going to stroll along and do it while you sit there in your recliner rocker, watching television and sipping soda. As a commercial break comes you say, "Holy Ghost, now is Your chance," and you expect Him to move. No, you have to separate yourself, get hungry, cry out for Him. You have to pray.

Don't Die Without the Anointing

I know that I would rather die than not have the anointing. If God told me I couldn't walk in His anointing, then I would ask Him to take me home, because there would be nothing else to live for.

God wants to make us vessels that He can flow through. But you have to cry out to Him. "God, I desire to be used of You. I want so badly to be used of You. Use me, Lord. Use me, O God, use me!" Then He will come and He will use you.

Some people don't believe this. They think they can say, "God, You are looking for someone with all these qualifications. Well, I have this degree and this diploma. You really can't do without me. If You don't take me, Your kingdom will suffer. God, if You don't have me, You know the world will suffer. I'm indispensable!"

Yes, God wants you. But God can do without you. Don't ever think that without you, heaven will close down or without you, God will resign and leave the throne. He already left heaven once, when He came here to die for mankind, and rose again.

Are You Hungry?

There must be a hunger. The Word says, "The effectual fervent prayer of a righteous man availeth much" (James 4:16). There is a story about a certain man by the name of Brainerd who would lie face down in the snow and pray. The snow, for meters around him, would melt because of the fervor of his praying.

People don't want to do that today. They will "pray" in a room where the television is on, so that they can watch the ballgame while they are praying. Call a church barbecue and watch them come by the hundreds — but call a prayer meeting, perhaps an all-night prayer meeting, and listen to the excuses. "I'm so tired, Pastor. I've been working all week."

You must want the Holy Ghost. You must thirst for Him. You must desire the anointing more than anything else in life. You must want it more than you want life itself. You have to mean business with God; get serious with God. It is not a quick stroll down the aisle to have a hand slapped on your head. You have to desire it, intensely desire it from the bottom of your heart and from the depths of your being. You cry out to God, "Do whatever You have to do, but please, let me be a part of it. Do a work in my heart!" God can do a work in your heart.

Look What Happened to Saul

God will work on some people like He did on Saul in Acts 9. He knocked Saul clean off his horse and made him blind for three days and nights. Some people who totally oppose God will be dealt with like that.

I have never had something like that come my way. Neither has the majority of us. Generally, it happens to those who have desired it and called out for it.

Read the life stories of some of the great men of God such as A.A. Allen. He locked himself in a room, and told his wife not to let him out, even if he screamed. When he eventually walked out of that room, the glory of God was all over him. He was anointed with fresh oil!

Everyone wants a ministry, but no one wants to pay the price to become the vessel God wants. When we become hungry enough to do whatever it takes, God will fill us with fresh oil.

Chapter 10
The Powers of the World to Come

For it is impossible for those who were once enlightened, and have tasted of the heavenly gift, and were made partakers of the Holy Ghost,

And have tasted the good word of God, and the powers of the world to come,

If they shall fall away, to renew them again unto repentance; seeing they crucify to themselves the Son of God afresh, and put him to an open shame.

Hebrews 6:4-6

When you get enlightened, it means you have been born again. The light comes in. The heavenly gift this scripture passage speaks of is the Holy Spirit.

I do not want to go into a big theological explanation on whether someone can or cannot lose their salvation. This is a passage of scripture that has intrigued me ever since I first read it in the Word of God.

The line I want to focus on here is something that is also of great interest to me because of what God is doing in our meetings. It's the little line, "the powers of the world to come."

Come to the Paradise

I remember what happened when I was in Chicago in a Hispanic Church. We must have had about a thousand people that night. The power of God was all over them. People were lying all over the floor and I was speaking in other tongues.

Someone ran up to me and said, "You're speaking perfect Spanish." I thought to myself, *Well, I don't speak Spanish.* I've never learned to speak Spanish. I'd love to; it's a beautiful language, but I've never learned to speak it.

So I said, "What did I say?" He said, "You invited all the people to come down and come to paradise. You kept walking up and down, pointing to the people saying, 'Come to the paradise, come to the paradise.'"

The Joy of the Holy Ghost

We were in a meeting in Pittsburgh, Pennsylvania in January of 1990, and the glory of the Lord was in the place. Most of the people were not in their seats. They were lying on the floor under the power of God.

The presence of God came in like a cloud and people were filled with joy. It was bubbling out of their bellies. People were totally drunk in the Holy Ghost. The anointing of God was on them and they were in a place of total Holy Ghost ecstasy, total joy. They were beside themselves.

The Lord spoke to me and said, "You are tasting the powers of the world to come. This is a little bit of heaven, a glimpse of heaven, a glimpse of glory."

In other words, He was telling me, "You can't see it, but on that individual is My glory. The cloud of God is resting on a person. There is a little bit of heaven. A small portion of My glory has come down and rested on them."

Now it doesn't make sense to the other folks in the room because they're not under that. But if they got under that, they couldn't care what makes sense and what doesn't make sense.

If you come in and try to analyze or try to work out what's happening in these meetings with your mind, you'll miss it. Every time I stand in these meetings, I'm amazed at what God is doing. I leave these services totally amazed at what the Lord has done.

It All Began When We Got Hungry for God to Move

It started taking place in April of 1989. I had to make adjustments in my ministry. I didn't ask God that these things would begin to happen. I just said, "Lord, I am so hungry to see Your power displayed to touch people's lives. Please move. Do whatever You want to do."

We were in a series of meetings in Albany, New York. It was the time we began to have two meetings per day. Both my wife and I were hungry for God to move. We had such a desire to see the glory of the Lord made manifested.

I remember the Tuesday morning meeting. As I was preaching, the glory of the Lord came into the building. I felt it just like someone put a heavy blanket upon me and the presence of the Lord filled the house.

A lady was sitting about three rows back and I noticed she was blinking and looking at the ceiling. I stopped what I was doing and said, "Lady, what is wrong?" She told me nothing was wrong.

Then she said that as she was sitting there, she saw a thick fog or mist, like a cloud, come down and fill the room. The lights and the ceiling disappeared. It reminded her of growing up in a coastal town where in the early hours of the morning the mist was so thick you could only see a few feet in front of you.

I did not see this cloud, but I felt it. At that time, I called two people from the sound booth and they came walking down the aisle. When they got two-thirds of the way down the aisle, they fell under the power of God. No one touched them. Later they informed me that as they were walking down the aisle, they walked into a thick fog or mist and fell out under the power with not even a hand being laid upon them.

The Most Amazing Thing Happened

While I was preaching, the power of God began to fall. Many people began to fall out of their seats. It looked like someone was shooting them and in some places whole rows at a time would go down. They were laughing and crying and falling all over the place and looked like drunken people.

I tried to preach above the noise of the people but to no avail. The glory of the Lord fell in such a wonderful way. Some were healed in their seats. The Lord then said to me, "I will move all the time if you will allow Me to."

The move of God has continued since April 1989, until the time of this writing, July 1992. It is safe to say, without exaggeration, that about 100,000 people have been touched personally by this wonderful move of God we are still experiencing. In the past six months, over 8,000 people have been saved and about 4,000 have been baptized in water.

Ministers are arising who have been set ablaze by the glory resulting in revival spreading and churches growing. Some churches have grown from 100 to 600 in one year following the revivals. Others just in a space of one year have exploded by thousands. Many are growing at an incredible rate because of the move of God.

This Is Just like Heaven

I was in another meeting and was walking around the church praying for several folk as I felt prompted by the Lord. When I went to pray for a dear brother sitting to the left of me, he stood up and hugged me. Then he told me that he had died several years ago and had left his body for a time and was caught up into glory.

He said he knew what was happening was real because he had witnessed that same presence of the Holy Ghost — the glory of God — when he crossed over to the other side. When you cross over into the glory realm, you find that heaven is a place of great rejoicing.

Heaven is a place where there's no depression, no sadness, no sickness, no poverty, none of that. Heaven is a glorious place. The scripture says, "In thy presence is fulness of joy" (Psalm 11:16). That's what is in His presence.

According to Hebrews 6, I can be enlightened — born again. Then I can taste of the heavenly gift and be made a partaker of the Holy Ghost. I can also taste of the good Word of God, and the powers of the world to come.

It is possible to be enlightened, but never be made a partaker of the Holy Ghost. It is also possible to be made a partaker of the Holy Ghost, but never have tasted of the good Word of God. Or one could have tasted the good Word of God, but never have entered into the powers of the world to come. There is a progression in this scripture. I would think that babes in Christ have not entered into the deeper things of God.

It Is Time to Grow Into Maturity

This scripture is talking about maturity, growing up. We don't want to be big babies. It's only as you spend time in His presence on a day-by-day basis that you begin to mature. You stop being like a little bird with your mouth always open, waiting for the worm. When you've grown, you're the one carrying the worm and feeding others. You've learned how to get it yourself.

Sometimes when the power of God comes on me, I lose touch with the natural and the supernatural becomes so real to me. There have been times when I thought I would go home to be with the Lord. The glory was so on me that it was lifting me into another realm, the realm of God. I wanted to be with Him more than I wanted to be down here.

I began to realize the meaning of some of the songs written many years ago such as, "Turn Your Eyes Upon Jesus." I realized that the writer of that song had experienced such a realm of glory so that everything in the earth "grew strangely dim." I began to understand the song that said, "It is joy unspeakable and full of glory, and the half has never yet been told."

It Is a Joy Unspeakable and Full of Glory

I discovered that when the glory came on me, I couldn't speak. Then I realized why it was unspeakable. You get beside yourself. You get almost to the point where if people didn't know what was happening, they would think you were drunk. You're just intoxicated on the Holy Ghost.

> For whether we be beside ourselves, (mad, as some say) it is to God (and concerns Him): or whether we be sober (in our right mind), it is for your cause (benefit).

> **2 Corinthians 5:13**

The Lord said to me one time, "It's not your job to convince people that this is from Me. It's not your job to try to force people to accept it. All I want you to do is set a table before them and let them come and eat." And I remembered the scripture, "O taste and see that the Lord is good" (Psalm 34:8).

I am talking about entering into that place. You would feel very offended if you set a table for guests and just before they got to the table they turned and walked away. So God is saying to the Church, "Come and eat. If you don't eat, I'm going to find other people who will come and eat."

Not a One-Time Experience

If tasting of the powers of the world to come was a one-time experience, then all you would need is a one-time experience. You'd never need to come in a prayer line again. You'd never need prayer. You'd never need to enter into that place.

But you know what? I'm convinced in my heart this is a constant process for every child of God. We should daily be filled with the Holy Ghost. We should daily let the Spirit of God come on us. We should daily taste of the good things of the Lord.

If you would come to God daily, you wouldn't have that depression like you've been having. Your life will be filled and out of your belly will flow rivers of living water. It is a little bit of heaven — just a little bit of heaven.

Lord, I pray, let heaven come down upon every one who reads this book. As the song says, let heaven come down and glory fill every soul.

Chapter 11
The Abuse of the Anointing

What bothered me in my studies of the lives of the great men and women of God was that many of them paid a horrible price in their personal lives. Many lost their children because they were never around for them while they were obeying the call. Or their marriage came apart because they spent very little time building a solid relationship on a firm foundation meant to last a lifetime.

I was direct in my prayer to the Lord when I told Him, "Lord, I am not prepared to lose my wife or my kids over the ministry. You gave them to me as a responsibility. If it doesn't work at home, why export it?"

So Heavenly Minded, No Earthly Good

Some ministers have neglected the things of everyday life in order to get into a superspiritual world. They have no relationships with anyone. I personally know men who have no one to speak honestly into their lives. They are surrounded by "yes" people who tell them what they want to hear and who only stay around them to boost their insecurities and their inferiority complexes.

Why Have the Mighty Fallen?

Why is it that many great men of God are blown out of the water? Is it because they cannot handle the power of God? I know that many have touched the gold and the glory and have been eaten up by worms like Herod in Acts 12.

We only have to look at the lives of Saul, David, and Samson, to name a few, to see some of the things that will bring people down. The enemy knows that the only way to stop an individual from achieving great things in God is to render them powerless and ineffective in their Christian walk and testimony by coming against them in three areas.

> **Love not the world, neither the things that are in the world. If any man love the world, the love of the Father is not in him.**
>
> **For all that is in the world, the lust of the flesh, the lust of the eyes, and the pride of life, is not of the Father, but is of the world.**
>
> **And the world passeth away, and the lust thereof: but he that doeth the will of God abideth forever.**
>
> **1 John 2:15-17**

Pitfall One: The Lust of the Flesh Lifestyles of the Rich and Famous

Many of God's chosen have become money-minded and have lost the anointing. They preach for money and do things in the ministry with a money motive behind it instead of a ministry motive behind it.

It is so important to realize that money follows ministry. If you meet people's needs, they will meet your needs. I know of one preacher in particular who is only concerned about having a meeting somewhere and selling his books. He thinks he is doing what God wants him to do, not realizing that he is prostituting the anointing on his life.

Many ministers will not preach unless they are guaranteed a certain amount, plus air fares, plus, plus, plus. That is why we, in our ministry, pay our own expenses and take our own offerings.

Now I am the first one to admit that there is abuse on both sides. Either the abuse of the ministry by the people, or the abuse of the people by the ministry. Don't label all in the ministry as charlatans because of the excesses of the few.

It's amazing how it's always the ones who are doing nothing for God who know how it should be done. There are ministries that start off exposing the cults but then turn on the Body of Christ like cannibals. They build their ministries off the failings of God's servants.

Excesses in the Message

God's servants should be blessed according to the scripture. He takes pleasure in the prosperity of His servants and those who labor in the Word should be worthy of double honor. But instead of being moderate, many parade themselves like Hollywood stars, flying around in corporate jets, indulging in lavish lifestyles.

Now I have no problem with a ministry that is in demand having a plane. But there is so much waste in many ministries with giant mailing lists and crises letters, fleecing the Body of Christ, using every available gimmick from anointing oil to holy water. I personally think those days are over in the Body of Christ.

The tithe should go to the local church and the local churches should get behind the traveling missionary or evangelist. This would solve many of the excesses that have arisen in the Body of Christ.

Some ministers have adopted the erroneous modus operandi of "find a need and fill it" which has given birth to giant Ishmaels in the Body of Christ. They will forever speak of man's ability to dream and create, but that does not mean it was instituted by God.

The Clash of the Titans

The battle has been for many years between pastors and evangelists fighting for their piece of the pie. In many instances, it revolves around money. How many times I've left a church knowing that I was ripped off in the offerings. They played Ananias and Sapphira with me and kept back part of the offerings, telling me there were a lot of expenses.

Instead of going for a full-out revival, and working together as one powerful force for God, the evangelist and the pastor are working against each other. In many instances the evangelist is ripped off and says nothing. Or he goes para-church and begins his own crusades, at least knowing that the expenses were his. Then he is shocked to find the extra money is there to pay the expenses and move ahead in the ministry.

Many are critical of evangelists and make them out to be money-grabbing charlatans. Yet in some cases, they were forced to resort to questionable tactics in order to survive.

Competition in the Ministry

Evangelist against evangelist is also a battle that has been around from the days of the tent revivals to the present. Games of "my tent is bigger than your tent" to "my television ministry is bigger than yours" are not uncommon. Competition instead of compassion is the driving force behind them. Crusades can be purchased in third world countries for a fee of one dollar per head.

They bring a guaranteed crowd of one hundred thousand. Not bad, when you realize it looks good on television.

There are mailing lists that in some circles can be purchased for a fee from agencies that also control Christian media. They will help you get on 100 markets and at the end of the month will squeeze you for $250,000. The result is often partner appeal letters that create crisis after crisis such as "we had a bad winter," or "if you don't give, we are going off the air." Or those evangelists build another white elephant and the public only gives to brick and mortar.

Evangelists and pastors are taking shots at each other from their pulpits because of spiritual jealousy and insecurities. They end up fighting for ratings like some late-night talk show competing for survival in this dog-eat-dog world we are living in.

We Have Brought the World into the Church Instead of Taking the Church into the World

If God cannot trust us with unrighteous mammon — money — which represents power and glory, how can He trust us with the true riches of heaven? No wonder the Church does not see the power of God displayed as it was seen in the book of Acts.

The Church makes excuses for its backslidden lifestyle of compromise and worldliness. The result is that the world is getting involved in the Church in the area of discipline. We are being corrected by the world for what we are doing. This, dear friends, is an indictment on the Body of Christ.

You Cannot Buy the Anointing

Some even think they can buy the anointing. There are the multimillionaire businessmen seeking to purchase and control the servant of God through new cars and Rolex watches and expensive jewelry. They follow the man of God like blood-sucking groupies. They are a part of the enemy's plot to control the servant of God.

Instead of just giving money with no strings attached, they want recognition and reserved seating at major conventions. Yet they need to repent and hit the altar. They must come to the realization that they need Jesus.

Another problem group is the small carnal-minded deacon boards who hold meetings to argue over whether they should spend the extra money to buy two-ply instead of one-ply toilet paper for the restroom of the church. They have no problem earning good money, but they balk at the idea of giving their pastor a raise. They would rather pray, "Lord, You keep him humble and we'll keep him poor."

The Games Some Preachers Play

Even in the ministry, there is often more politics than in Washington or Ten Downing Street. If you want to preach at a certain church, then you are not allowed to preach at another one because the pastor doesn't agree with the minister of the church you are going to. In short, you have to play all the political games if you want to get anywhere in the ministry.

In some instances you have to be a social climber — someone who reaches for success by compromising his heart-felt principles. Friendships that are only based on what you can get out of an individual. When he doesn't produce, then he is cut off like a gangrenous limb and treated like a leper.

Groups of churches that are banded together denote power. If you don't play religious ball with the hierarchy, then in a mafia-type operation, they will put a contract out on your ministry and suddenly doors that were once opened are now closed. People who you once were in fellowship with suddenly will have nothing to do with you.

The word is out as spiritual mafia hit men go out of their way to destroy another man's life and ministry. Lies about his personal life and lies over his doctrine have caused the downfall of many a man of God and has hindered the cause of Christ greatly.

It All Revolves Around Jealousy

It is a "Cain and Abel" scenario that is being played out between ministers and ministries. The thought that God might accept one above the others is too much for some to accept. They seek to destroy one another with every available means.

I have watched with a heavy heart as two anointed men of God will resort to tactics "by hook or by crook" to destroy one another. No wonder the Church is weak and has no anointing.

Since when does God give the right to an individual to be the watch dog of the Church and to bite and devour one another for the protection of the gospel. It is incredible to see what is being done in the name of the gospel. If I did some of those things, I would not be able to sleep at night let alone get behind the pulpit and proclaim the gospel. I wonder how some can pray with a clean heart before God. Oh, how the Church needs to have such a Holy Ghost revival that we fall in love with Jesus and then in love with each other.

I have purposed in my heart that I will not compromise or play games. There is only one whom I bow my knee to and who has rule in my life and His name is Jesus, my Lord and Savior. Let us have the genuine once again and go back to the days of Charles Finney and

Smith Wigglesworth — the days of the power of God made manifest among men.

The Leprosy of Namaan Has Come to the Church

But he went in, and stood before his master. And Elisha said unto him, Whence comest thou, Gehazi? And he said, Thy servant went no whither.

And he said unto him, Went not mine heart with thee, when the man turned again from his chariot to meet thee? Is it time to receive money, and to receive garments, and olive-yards, and vineyards, and sheep, and oxen, and menservants, and maidservants?

The leprosy therefore of Naaman shall cleave unto thee, and unto thy seed for ever. And he went out from his presence a leper as white as snow.

2 Kings 5:25-27

The leprosy of Namaan has come to the Body of Christ. They have sought after the riches of this world in exchange for what should be done in the service of the King of kings.

It is not that God will not bless and prosper His people. On the contrary, He delights in the prosperity of His servants. But when an individual ministers out of a heart motive for financial gain rather than to see people saved, healed, and set free, this is a slur against the cross of Jesus Christ.

For ye know the grace of our Lord Jesus Christ, that, though he was rich, yet for your sakes he became poor, that ye through his poverty might be rich.

2 Corinthians 8:9

It is one thing to be blessed of the Lord. It is another thing to go out of your way to look for material blessings as the main purpose of ministry.

An elderly statesman in the Body of Christ, who for over fifty years gave his life in foreign missions, asked the Lord why he had nothing materially to show for fifty years on the missionfield.

Others had established themselves so that if they never preached another day in the ministry they would retire as millionaires. The Lord spoke to him and said, "Son, they chose their reward down here below, while yours is waiting for you in heaven."

I Believe in Prosperity

I believe in prosperity and the blessing of God. I not only preach it, but live in the realm of blessing. So I am not against God's blessing. I am against carnal, wrongly motivated individuals — whether in the ministry or out of the ministry — who manipulate the move of God and make merchandise out of the ministry.

Pitfall Two: The Pride of Life
Pride Comes Before the Fall

Most of those who fall through pride did not start out that way. Over the years, from the beginning of their ministries, they endured hardships and tough times. Instead of that producing character in their lives, they became bitter towards God and bitter towards the flock of God. Many end up as wrecks along the highway of life. This, of course, is pride in some form or another.

Others arrive at their goal and because they have endured hardships in the early stage of their ministry, now they pamper themselves with worldly goods. They say to themselves, *I am worth it. After all, I am a pastor of the largest church in the state.*

Some are in pride over their great humility. Others are in pride over the size of their church and they play childish games of "my church is bigger than your church." In attending some conferences, they prance around in their $3,000 suits with their heads held high. They are too mighty to condescend to men of low estate as though they would be infected with a virus and lose their anointing.

Others need the protection of their body guards, usually a muscle-bound Kung Fu expert who has about as much brains and spirituality as a chicken. Psalm 23 and Psalm 91 have lost their power for them. What protection they have is coming from the arm of flesh.

Let This Mind Be in You

Pride keeps man from seeing clearly. The Bible says, "Let this mind be in you, which was also in Christ Jesus...He humbled himself, and became obedient unto death, even the death of the cross" (Philippians 2:5, 8). The Word of God declares, "to every man that is among you, not to think of himself more highly than he ought to think, but to think soberly" (Romans 12:3). We are not to think like some third-world dictator whose power has gone to his head.

Others allow pride to come in through their education. The more degrees they have, the more they distance themselves from the Body of Christ. They become nothing more than brain-bound ministers communicating a gospel that they themselves have a hard time understanding.

Pride comes in when an individual thinks he is responsible for what God is doing through his life. He tries to take the glory because he thinks he is doing the work.

Pride caused the fall of Lucifer. He said, "I will exalt my throne above the stars of God" (Isaiah 14:13). It is interesting to note that the original sin is still causing problems in the Body of Christ.

Pitfall Three: The Lust of the Eyes

We could focus on many different things under this category. But I would like to discuss another area that the enemy has used effectively to destroy a ministry. It is the area of a break-up in marriages of great men of God. Men have fallen into adultery or sexual perversion.

Many would ask why some would even want to negate all the good that a man might have done for God by speaking of his weaknesses. We must realize everyone has potential weaknesses. The Bible says that even Elijah was a man subject to like passions as we are (James 5:17). Just because God uses an individual does not mean that he cannot fall into a snare if he doesn't lay a good foundation.

We have a habit of putting a man on a pedestal instead of realizing that it is all Jesus. The Western world, especially in the United States, wants its superstars, its spiritual heros. Then they are disillusioned when they see these men fall and realize they have feet of clay.

A Solid Marriage Equals a Solid Ministry

It is not good that man should be alone so God made the woman to be his help and to stand by his side (Genesis 2:18). Many ministers, instead of building a strong relationship with their wives, allow things to merely exist. They go through life with an unhappy marriage, usually something that was a mistake from the beginning.

Every effort should be made to make your wife or husband your best friend. I thank God every day for my wife. She is my best friend and she can do for me what no other woman can do. I would rather be with her than any other human being on the face of the earth.

There seems to be a lack of commitment in the Church today concerning marriage. If the slightest pressure arises, people split up and say, "Well, it just didn't work out."

Marriage Is Honorable and the Bed Undefiled

In some cases, ministers' wives have a puritanical attitude towards sex. Many of them grew up thinking sex was dirty and that you could not be spiritual and have the anointing on your life and still take care of the sexual side of a marriage. They neglect that side until it is too late and they find someone has taken their place. They wonder why the devil destroyed their marriage. But it died because of neglect and had nothing to do with the devil.

There is nothing more spiritual in a marriage than a bunch of flowers, a candlelight dinner, and a night of passion between two (married to each other) lovers devoted to each other for the rest of their lives.

Men, the most spiritual thing you can do in your marriage is to take care of your wives. And the same goes for the wives. Take care of your husbands. If you don't, someone else will.

Chapter 12
How to Maintain the Anointing

The Importance of Rest

Some might ask, "Can an individual be anointed and enjoy life?" I say we can. You've heard the saying that all work and no play makes Johnny a dull boy. Rest and recreation are important. Jesus said to the disciples, "Come ye yourselves apart into a desert place, and rest awhile" (Mark 6:31).

Some men have boasted of having no hobbies and sports. Yet they are caught in a motel somewhere with a hobby that costs them their ministries. Others work constantly without taking a vacation. They end up physically and mentally tired and open themselves up to an attack of the enemy.

Rest and recreation are so important. I find this especially true because we are on the road constantly in crusades, preaching an average of 450 meeting per annum. We take a break midway in the year. Then in December, we spend time resting, playing with the kids, and spending time together. I don't even go near a meeting if I can help it. When the new year begins, I come back with the eye of the tiger.

It is actually better during the year to take frequent short breaks than one long one. In this way, you can keep your mind clear. A mind and body that is tired is not a yielded vessel through which the Holy Spirit can flow. Learning to rest in the Lord and to quit striving and doing things in the flesh is something that has helped me.

There is a teaching on burn-out that I don't believe in — but not because burn-out doesn't happen. I believe if you obey God and do what He wants you to do, He will sustain you. The burn-out comes from ministry in the flesh that usually gives birth to an Ishmael.

Times of Refreshing

When the times of refreshing shall come from the presence of the Lord.

Acts 3:19b

There is a question in the hearts of God's people many times about the anointing. They say, "It is wonderful to go to a revival meeting and get touched by the anointing. It is wonderful to experience the presence of God. But how do I maintain it in my life?"

Too many people think it's not possible to keep the anointing. "You do not know my circumstances," they will say. "If you knew my husband, then you would know I could never be anointed of God all the time. Brother, Rodney, you don't know my wife. My mother-in-law just moved into the house. You don't know what circumstances we are living under. If you saw my car, you would realize that I can never be anointed of God and drive that car."

Everyone has a giant in their life that they must face. Something screams at them every day. It tries to rob them of the blessing of God in their life. But giants can be brought down.

The Fruit of Patience

We have to learn — regardless of the giants, the problems, and the trials and tests of life that come to everyone — that we can remain constant. One of the fruit of the spirit is patience. That means to be constantly the same way all the time.

A lot of Christians are up one day, down the next. They are like a yo-yo Christian. One day they are on a high and if they are on a high, it is wonderful. But the next day they are on a low. You never know where they are going to be.

Hebrews 13:8 says, "Jesus Christ the same yesterday, and to day, and for ever." God is always the same. God doesn't wake up in the morning depressed. God doesn't walk around the throne room with His hands behind His back saying, "Oh, my arthritis is killing Me. Where is my walking stick?" Then He looks around and says, "I don't know what we are going to do? Jesus has pneumonia, a third of the angels have the Hong Kong flu, and I have to hock the pearly gates today to make a payment on the throne room." No, God is not that way and neither should we be.

Taking Control Over Your Circumstances

Yet, we are living down here in the earth. We are subject to circumstances about us, sometimes that seem to be beyond our control. But every circumstance is not beyond our control. We can take authority over those circumstances. What the Lord wants to teach us is that we need to get to a place in God where we can stay anointed, live anointed, and still be married and have children and conduct business affairs.

Some people say you can't be anointed of God and be married. People think if God is going to use you, you just can't have a wife and kids. But I want you to know that God has ordained marriage and God has ordained children. You can be anointed with three or five or ten kids. You better be anointed with ten! You can be anointed and walking in the presence of God. It is a decision you make every day.

Two Choices to Make

When you get out of bed, you have two choices. I am either going to walk in the presence of God today, or I am going to go after the flesh. Every time you come against a circumstance and someone riles you and gets you mad, you can say, "I am either going to react in the flesh, or I am going to act in the spirit."

You can be anointed and still be you. People have the idea that if you are anointed, you walk on a cloud, harps are playing, all around are angels, and you don't even go to the restroom because you are so anointed. You float along and miracles happen all over the place. People jump out of wheelchairs when you walk by. It is not the case.

Everyone Faces a Giant

Did you know that Smith Wigglesworth had kidney stones for six years? He would have powerful miracles and signs and wonders in his meetings. But sometimes he would have to run off the platform in the middle of the service to go to the bathroom. They say he passed around a hundred and fifty-six kidney stones during a six-year period.

In total agony he would lie in the hotel room and roll on the floor. Then he would get up and go to the meeting. People would get healed miraculously, but in his own life, he faced the greatest trial of his life — total pain. Yet he was anointed of God.

Such a trial would sideline most people. "How are you today?" "Oh, my stomach is still giving me trouble." Well, get out there and raise the dead. Get out there and get people healed. Get your eyes off yourself and forget about the way you feel.

There are times when I don't feel like ministering because I've been running hard and fast, going to bed at two or three o'clock in the morning. The last thing I feel like doing is getting out of bed and crawling into a service. I don't feel like looking at a bunch of dead people in some places, trying to get them revived.

It Takes a Quality Decision

You make a decision. There are times that you wake up in the morning and you get out of bed and you make a decision. "I will walk in the anointing of God today. This is the day that the Lord has made; I will rejoice and be glad in it."

We will face every challenge. We will face every obstacle in the name of Jesus. We will face it head on. We are going to face it by the anointing of God and we are going to stay anointed. It is a decision you make. You can roll over and play dead or you can rise up in Jesus' name and tell the devil where to go.

People say, "How can I stay anointed?" You can. There are many ways that God has provided in His Word that we can stay on the cutting edge. We can stay sharp. We can stay in tune.

You are not going to stay anointed if you slip back into your pit of depression and do nothing but watch television. No, the way to deal with a situation is not to hide yourself away for a couple of days. When you come out, it is going to be even worse. The way to deal with it is to confront it head on and say, "We are going to change this situation. We are going to change the circumstances."

The Prayer of Repentance

If we are going to be anointed, the one thing we have to do is repent. Repent. One thing that a child of God should be able to do more than anything is repent. You know First John 1:9 says, "If we confess our sins, he is faithful and just to forgive us our sins, and to cleanse us from all unrighteouness."

Do you know that verse was not written for the sinner. I am hearing some evangelists telling the sinners, "If you confess your sins, He is faithful and just to forgive you." That is not written for the sinners. First of all, if the sinner comes who has been unsaved for forty years, and he confesses his sins, he is going to have to confess for forty years. He has a lot of sins to confess.

That verse is written to the born-again believer. First John was written to the Church. If *we* confess our sins, He is faithful and just to forgive us our sins and to cleanse us from all unrighteousness. That covers all types of sins. That covers the sins of omission and the sins of commission; the sins that you know about and the sins you don't know about.

Sometimes you offend people without ever realizing you did it. But if you repent, God forgives you, washes you, cleanses you. That is why you better not walk around criticizing people. They might be walking in repentance and while you are criticizing them, you are criticizing the blood of Jesus. Repent, the Bible says. If we want to be anointed of God, we need to repent.

Do Not Deceive Yourselves

Some people want to pull the wool over God's eyes. They are walking in unforgiveness. They are walking in strife. They are walking in bitterness. They are walking in pride and they come and sit in church and they want the blessings of God. They want the anointing of God. The Lord can't anoint that. God is not going to anoint sin. God is not going to anoint the flesh. God is not going to anoint some little lying devil.

You look at some pastors and realize why they never see a move of God in their church. They talk, but they never fulfill their talk. All of it is politics, to be honest with you.

God is not going to anoint a heart that is not a heart of integrity. God cannot anoint a heart that is not pure. God cannot anoint a heart that has ulterior motives. God cannot anoint a heart like Simon the sorcerer who said to Peter, "Give me this power." He wanted to buy it. He wanted to pay money for it.

Peter said, "Thy money perish with thee, because thou hast thought that the gift of God may be purchased with money. Thou hast neither part nor lot in this matter: for thy heart is not right in the sight of God" (Acts 8:19-21).

God Anoints the Truth

God wasn't going to anoint Simon the sorcerer. Then you realize why the Church is dead. God cannot anoint a lie. You think, *If the pastor has no integrity, God have mercy on the poor congregation. They don't stand a chance.*

Chapter 13
The Ministry of Laying on of Hands

Therefore leaving the principles of the doctrine of Christ, let us go on unto perfection; not laying again the foundation of repentance from dead works, and of faith toward God,

Of the doctrine of baptisms, and of laying on of hands.

Hebrews 6:1, 2

The laying on of hands is one of the doctrines of Christ. If we would see Bible results, we must follow Bible principles.

And he said unto them, Go ye into all the world, and preach the gospel to every creature.

He that believeth and is baptized shall be saved; but he that believeth not shall be damned.

And these signs shall follow them that believe; In my name shall they cast out devils; they shall speak with new tongues;

They shall take up serpents; and if they drink any deadly thing, it shall not hurt them; they shall lay hands on the sick, and they shall recover.

So then after the Lord had spoken unto them, he was received up into heaven, and sat on the right hand of God.

And they went forth, and preached every where, the Lord working with them, and confirming the word with signs following.

Mark 16:15-20

If It's Good Enough for Jesus, Then It's Good Enough for Me

In His ministry, Jesus ministered by the laying on of hands. It is one of the principles of the doctrine of the Lord Jesus Christ. Every time I teach on it, in my own heart, I realize how special this is. It is such a holy thing that we do when we lay hands on people. It's something that should not to be taken lightly. I believe the Spirit of God is grieved many times by what is being done in the Church under the guise of laying on of hands.

It is not just symbolic; there is an actual transfer of the anointing. As I read the Bible, I begin to see the true story. I begin to see that when Jesus touched people, something happened. When the woman with an issue of blood came and touched the hem of His garment, virtue flowed out of Jesus into her and she was healed. There was an actual transference.

I begin to see that even under the Old Testament, the patriarchs of old conferred blessing upon their children by laying hands upon them. They spoke by the gift of faith and transferred on their children the blessing that would be upon them for the rest of their lives. It came to pass even as their fathers said.

Even when the scapegoat was taken, hands were laid upon that scapegoat. The sins of the children of Israel were transferred onto that goat and then it was sent out. I begin to see that there is a transference, an impartation, that comes with the laying on of hands.

Empty Hands on Empty Heads

One of the things I am cautious of, and try to tell people, is that you can lay hands on people all the time, but if you have nothing to give, what is going to happen? If you have empty hands, what are you doing? You are only putting empty hands on empty heads. We want to get our hands full.

The Bible says, "We have this treasure in earthen vessels" (Second Corinthians 4:7). By the same token the anointing of God can be in a building, it can be tangible, but because there is no one there placing the demand upon that anointing, nothing happens.

There must have been many other sick people in the days of the woman with the issue of blood, yet she alone was the one who received her healing that day. Many others touched Jesus, but she alone touched Him with faith and when she touched Him, she was made whole. She placed a demand on the anointing of the ministry of Jesus. Virtue flowed out. Dunamis power flowed out of Jesus into her body.

You Have to Place a Demand on the Anointing

When hands are laid upon us, we expect something to happen. Don't come in the prayer line if you don't expect anything to happen. Many people come in the lines who don't even know what's going on. They don't know the principle behind the ministry of laying on of hands.

I understand that you can lay hands on in faith — every believer can pray in faith — but there is a ministry of laying on of hands. Every believer can pray for people. Every believer can lay their hands on someone, pray the prayer of faith, and trust God for a mighty work. But there is a ministry of laying on of hands of impartation when men of God receive something from the Lord.

Paul received something from the Lord. He wrote to Timothy and said, "Neglect not the gift that is in thee, which was given thee by prophecy, with the laying on of the hands" (First Timothy 4:14). The gift was given by the laying on of hands.

I know that I have sat under anointed men of God and then said, "Lay hands on me. Let that anointing come on me. I want some of that anointing." I have watched the change in my life; I've seen the impartation. It may have been a new boldness that comes on me, or maybe flowing in a different realm.

Don't Let Just Anyone Lay Hands on You

You have to be careful who you allow to lay hands on you. You have to be careful whose ministry you sit under. That anointing will come onto you. There is a transference of anointing. That is why in the meetings, I do not allow just anyone to come up and start laying hands on people.

In fact, we have been in meetings where someone walked out the crowd and started laying hands on people. I said, "Sit down!" "Well I'm using this." I said, "Sit down!"

Now I am not trying to be horrible, but if they want to have their own meeting, let them go and get their own auditorium. Let the people come and then they can do what they want to do.

Laying hands on someone is more than just praying for that person. There is a transference of the anointing. We need to be careful that we know which is the Holy Ghost. We discern by the Spirit of God. We don't discern by our natural human reason, but we discern by the Spirit of God.

There Is a Ministry of Impartation

There is a ministry of impartation. There is a ministry of laying on of hands. It doesn't matter who the minister is, or how anointed that person is. It really doesn't matter if Jesus Christ of Nazareth Himself was standing there about to lay hands on people. If you don't come in faith to receive, you won't receive. The measure or the proportion of the faith that you come with to receive is the measure and the proportion of that which will be imparted to you.

If you come expecting nothing, you are going to leave with nothing. If you come and you are sick in your body, and hands are laid on you, and you don't really expect to be healed, then you will not be healed. Even if you are coming as a last resort because doctors have given you up to die, but you don't really expect anything to happen, you are going to die. Then people have the audacity to say, "You see, healing doesn't work. That man came for healing and he was prayed for and he went away and died."

I've got news for you; he was going to die anyway. He didn't believe God; he wasn't trusting God.

We pray in healing lines all the time. We are praying for people six days a week, twice a day. When you lay hands on people that often, you get a feel for the anointing. The moment you put your hand on someone, you can feel that anointing go right into them and come right back out of them. But the anointing doesn't even go into some people. It just bounces right off their unbelieving head. It is like laying hands on a refrigerator. It is like laying hands on a motor car door.

It is like laying hands on a dummy. You can look in their eyes and see the lights are on, but nobody is home. There is no demand placed upon the anointing. Some people receive immediately without you even touching them. You have to keep your hands on others for about ten or fifteen minutes just to break them through from the natural into the spiritual realm.

Some people need hands laid on them for about three hours in the hope that God would breathe some life into them so that they can become a living soul like He did with Adam, back in creation. He breathed into Adam the life of God. Some people need the life of God breathed into them.

Why Are the People Not Touched?

Different ministries are obviously disturbed about different things, but people with a healing ministry, are most disturbed about those who come to the services and leave sick. I have spoken to men in the healing ministry about this. If you have a healing ministry, you are disturbed by the fact that people would come in a wheelchair and leave in a wheelchair or that people would come sick and leave sick.

The thing that bothered me was that people would come to our meetings and yet would not be touched by the Spirit of God. In the middle of a mighty move of the Spirit of God, they would leave untouched. I couldn't understand that. I would go home from a meeting or go back to my hotel room and say, "God I don't understand it. Why can these poor people not be touched? Why can they not even feel your presence, Lord?"

In our meetings, the anointing of God is all over the place. Sometimes I can hardly stand; sometimes I can hardly speak because the anointing is so heavy. Others in the meetings have been hit by the power of God, yet people are sitting there, looking around, and they can't even feel the anointing.

"Lord what is going on here? What is happening?" The Lord said to me, "The reason some come in and never receive is because 99.99 percent of their thought life is far from Me. Their hearts are far from Me." Even though they go to church on Sunday and they carry a Bible big enough to choke a donkey, they are simply sitting in the pew. When that dry-cleaning service that they go to once a week is over, that is it.

Living in a Higher Realm

They slip back into their old lifestyle. They slip back into the strife; they slip back into the life of television. They slip back into a life of carnality and their thought life is far from God. That is why it is hard to walk into a service where the Holy Ghost is moving and try to enter into the Spirit. The flesh can't come into the Spirit. The flesh can't move into that place God has prepared.

There needs to come a breakthrough in your life. God will break you out of that old life of carnality and bring you into a life of walking in the Spirit.

There is a ministry of laying on of hands! In the Word of God you see that Jesus blessed the children. He imparted blessing to children when He laid His hands upon them (Matthew 19:13-15). He laid hands on the sick and healed them (Luke 4:40).

Then also we see the laying on of hands to ordain and anoint for ministry, to set apart for ministry. What really happens? When you take your hands, by the Spirit of God, and put it on somebody's head, the life of God on the inside of you flows out of you into them. There is no hype about it. You just do it. Sometimes Jesus didn't even pray; He just touched the people. You can go to someone lying in a hospital bed, dying of cancer, and put your hand on them and let the life of God flow out of you.

There Is a Transference

As a result of the laying on of hands, many will be healed and evil spirits and tormenting devils that were bothering them will leave. There is a transference. Either the anointing is there or it is not there. If it is not there, go home. If it is there, learn to flow with it.

Learn to co-operate with the anointing. If you minister to people you must mix faith with the fact that God has anointed you. That is the principal of laying on of hands. There is a transference. There is an impartation. The anointing is taken and the anointing is given.

The anointing of God can go into a cloth. In Acts 19:11, 12 the scripture says, "God wrought special miracles by the hands of Paul: So that from his body were brought unto the sick handkerchiefs or aprons, and the diseases departed from them, and evil spirits went out of them." The anointing of God can go into the cloth and then into an individual.

Faith on Both Sides of the Cloth

There must be faith on both sides of the cloth — faith from the minister ministering and faith from the individual receiving.

> And a certain woman, which had an issue of blood twelve years,
>
> And had suffered many things of many physicians, and had spent all that she had, and was nothing bettered, but rather grew worse,
>
> When she had heard of Jesus, came in the press behind, and touched his garment.
>
> For she said, If I may touch but his clothes, I shall be whole.

And straightway the fountain of her blood was dried up; and she felt in her body that she was healed of that plague.

And Jesus, immediately knowing in himself that virtue had gone out of him turned him about in the press, and said, Who touched my clothes?

And his disciples said unto him, Thou seest the multitude thronging thee, and sayest thou, Who touched me?

And he looked round about to see her that had done this thing.

But the woman fearing and trembling, knowing what was done in her, came and fell down before him, and told him all the truth.

And he said unto her, Daughter, thy faith hath made thee whole; go in peace, and be whole of thy plague.

Mark 5:25-34

One of the things that people in the Church all say is, "I am anointed." It is one thing to be anointed, but what are you going to do with the anointing when you get it? God doesn't anoint you so you can sit in a pew and look pretty. God anoints you for service in the Kingdom of God. He equips you for service and He blesses you so that you can bless others.

Cooperating with the Anointing

Whatever God does in your life is not so you can keep it to yourself. He wants you to give to others round about you. We have to understand the principle involved in the release of the anointing. Many people have a touch of God on their lives, but they don't know how to cooperate with or yield to the Spirit of God. They don't allow that anointing to flow forth from them to touch people round about them.

Sometimes, when you don't even expect it, God will move. I pray for people, and then I am amazed at what

133

happens when I pray for them. I have seen them picked up and thrown over three rows of chairs like a piece of rag. It shocks me. It is awesome.

I remember one time I prayed for a man, and the power of God came over my shoulder. It felt like a whirlwind. It picked him up off the ground, level with my waist, then it struck him to the ground. He saw it coming and he tried to duck out of the way. It was like a bolt of lightning hit the brother. I was shocked. As the power hit him, the first couple of rows all went out. It was like a Holy Ghost tornado came in there.

Awesome Displays of God's Power

We've seen awesome displays of God's power, awesome manifestations. I wish it could be like that all the time. Unfortunately — or maybe fortunately — it is not because people's faith is involved in it. The people who come are all at a different level of a hunger and thirst for God. They place a demand on that anointing. Many other people touched Jesus, but only one woman touched Him in faith. So, in every meeting it will be different.

One of the things the Lord impressed upon my heart was to demonstrate the transference of the anointing. That is what we are trying to do in the meetings to show people God's power. God might not use you in the same way that He uses me, but He can use you in different ways — in your home, laying hands on your children, in many different circumstances. It is so important that you understand this. Then you will be better equipped to minister to people when you realize that you are not going in your own strength.

Chapter 14
Message on the Anointing
Samson — A Type of the Church

And there was a certain man of Zorah, of the family of
the Danites, whose name was Manoah; and his wife
was barren, and bare not.

And the angel of the Lord appeared unto the woman,
and said unto her, Behold now, thou art barren, and bearest
not: but thou shalt conceive, and bear a son.

Now therefore beware, I pray thee, and drink not wine
nor strong drink, and eat not any unclean thing:

For, lo, thou shalt conceive, and bear a son; and no razor
shalt come on his head: for the child shall be a Nazarite unto
God from the womb: and he shall begin to deliver Israel out
of the hand of the Philistines.

Judges 13:2-5

Samson Was Called to a Special Ministry

Samson was called, appointed, and anointed by
God with a special and unique anointing. Samson had
an anointing to kill people. God had called Samson to
deliver His people and placed upon him an unusual
anointing. I don't believe we've seen anything like it
before or since. It was a unique anointing where the
glory of God would come upon him. Under the anointing of God, he would do great and wonderful things that
were beyond man's natural ability.

135

And the woman bare a son, and called his name Samson: and the child grew, and the Lord blessed him.

And the Spirit of the Lord began to move him at times in the camp of Dan between Zorah and Eshtaol.

Judges 13:24, 25

We see the anointing of God would come upon him and in a moment he would do extraordinary things under the power of God.

The Key to Samson's Anointing

Samson had to adhere to the Nazarite vow of no wine or strong drink. He would not visit a barber shop the whole of his life. He was to let his hair grow out long. No razor was to touch his head.

In Samson's life, there was a key to that anointing. In every individual, there is a key, a secret, and for each and every person it is a different thing. For Samson it was his hair. For you it might be something else. The Bible says that the Spirit of God would move on him at times. He would arise and enter into that which God had for him.

Reduced to the Point of His Fall

It is interesting to note that Samson is not remembered for his great ministry, but rather for his fall. If we asked people in the street or the shopping mall or wherever we went, "Do you know about Samson?" immediately the answer would come back, "Yes. I also know about Delilah."

This great man of God was reduced to the very thing that caused his fall. This is true of certain great men of God today. If we were to mention their names, many would forget about all of the wonderful things that God has done through their ministry and immediately reduce each man to the place, the time, and the date of his fall.

So Samson, for all of the years since his fall, is remembered by anyone who knows his story by a woman named Delilah. I believe in every child of God's life there is a Delilah. I'm not necessarily saying it's a woman. But a Delilah, nonetheless, is still a Delilah. For some it could be pride, for others it could be a temper, an anger, or something else that would control their lives.

The Enemy Wants to Steal the Anointing From Our Lives

Satan tries to come with these things to sap the very anointing from your life. He knows your weaknesses and he's had over 6,000 years of working on man to know your shortcomings. He knows just what buttons to push. He knows how to get you to react and he knows how to get you to walk in a place where the anointing of God can no longer rest upon your life. He wants to make you ineffective.

As long as Samson had his long hair, as long as Samson was under the anointing of God, he was unstoppable. City gates meant nothing to him; he would walk away with them. When you're under the anointing of God and you're walking in that place of the call of God, you are unstoppable in that which God has for your life.

But Samson had a big weakness in his life. He loved the world and he loved the things of the world. You can't have both. You can't have the anointing of God and the world. This is what people don't understand. They want to come to a meeting where the anointing of God is and the power of God begins to move and then go outside the door and carry on living like they did before.

You Cannot Live in Two Kingdoms

You cannot keep one foot in the world and one foot in the kingdom of God. If you can sit in a church and live a lifestyle that does not exemplify a child of God without feeling convicted then I want you to know the Holy Ghost is not a part of that place.

Samson was in bed with the world. Even though the anointing of God would rest upon him, the desire for the things of the flesh was greater in his life. Because of the awesomeness of the presence of God, he thought he could play with the world and get away with it. And he began to compromise.

> Then three thousand men of Judah went to the top of the rock Etam, and said to Samson, Knowest thou not that the Philistines are rulers over us? what is this that thou hast done unto us? And he said unto them, As they did unto me, so have I done unto them.
>
> And they said unto him, We are come down to bind thee, that we may deliver thee into the hands of the Philistines. And Samson said unto them, Swear unto me, that ye will not fall upon me yourselves.
>
> And they spake unto him, saying, No; but we will bind thee fast, and deliver thee into their hand: but surely we will not kill thee. And they bound him with two new cords, and brought him up from the rock.
>
> And when he came unto Lehi, the Philistines shouted against him: and the Spirit of the Lord came mightily upon him, and the cords that were upon his arms became as flax that was burnt with fire, and his bands loosed from off his hands.
>
> And he found a new jawbone of an ass, and put forth his hand, and took it, and slew a thousand men therewith.
>
> **Judges 15:11-15**

Playing with the Anointing

This was when he began to play with the anointing on his life. It is so dangerous to play with the anointing of God. He delivered himself into the hands of the Philistines, then broke the cords easily. He was mocking them, but in reality, he was setting himself up for his final undoing. He began to compromise what he believed. Many people compromise what they believe in order to be accepted.

Samson had a great anointing, but he played the fool and lost the anointing. Samson got to the place in his life that he thought he could do anything he wanted and get away with it. I'm convinced that men of God get to that place because of what God's doing in the ministry. Because of the anointing, the signs, the wonders, and the miracles, they get into the place where they think, *I can do anything I want.*

And if that's so for the men and women of God, how much is it for everyone in the Body of Christ? God blesses them just a little bit and they get to the place where they think, *I can do whatever I want.* No, you can't. Your life is not your own. You don't belong to you. You belong to the Most High God.

> **Then went Samson to Gaza, and saw there an harlot, and went in unto her.**
>
> **And it was told the Gazites, saying, Samson is come hither. And they compassed him in, and laid wait for him all night in the gate of the city, and were quiet all night, saying, In the morning, when it is day, we shall kill him.**
>
> **And Samson lay till midnight, and arose at midnight, and took the doors of the gate of the city, and the two posts, and went away with them, bar and all, and put them upon his shoulders, and carried them up to the top of an hill that is before Hebron.**
>
> **Judges 16:1-3**

The Prostitute and the Gates

The walls of some of the cities in those day were so wide, they could ride six or eight chariots on the top of them. So you can imagine how big the gates of the city were. This man has just been with a prostitute. He gets up out of bed, takes the city gates, and walks away with them. He says, "I'll show you. You lie in wait for me. I'm going to take your gates away."

> And it came to pass afterward, that he loved a woman in the valley of Sorek, whose name was Delilah.
>
> And the lords of the Philistines came up unto her, and said unto her, Entice him . . .
>
> Judges 16:4, 5

You see that's what the devil wants to do to you. He wants to entice you. He wants to draw you. He wants to lure you. He wants to get you to that place of compromise so that at your weakest time, he can destroy you.

> Entice him, and see wherein his great strength lieth (find out what the key is), and by what means we may prevail against him, that we may bind him to afflict him: and we will give thee every one of us eleven hundred pieces of silver.
>
> Judges 16:5

The Enemy Is Looking for the Key to the Anointing

> And Delilah said to Samson, Tell me, I pray thee, wherein thy great strength lieth and wherewith thou mightest be bound to afflict thee.
>
> And Samson said unto her, If they bind me with seven green withs that were never dried, then shall I be weak, and be as another man.
>
> Judges 16:6, 7

He knew that they could bind him with whatever they wanted to and they weren't going to hold him down. But in the back of his mind he's thinking, The last time they bound me, I snapped those cords and took a jawbone of a donkey and killed a thousand of them. Let's just play around with this. They can tie me up again. I'll just tease these people a little while, mock them. They think they're going to play with me. I'm the great Samson. I'm indestructible.

Then the lords of the Philistines brought up to her seven green withs which had not been dried, and she bound him with them.

Now there were men lying in wait, abiding with her in the chamber. And she said unto him, The Philistines be upon thee, Samson. And he brake the withs, as a thread of tow is broken when it toucheth the fire. So his strength was not known.

> **And Delilah said unto Samson, Behold, thou hast mocked me, and told me lies: now tell me, I pray thee, wherewith thou mightest be bound.**
>
> **Judges 16:8-10**

The devil will come at you constantly and he will try to find the key to the anointing on your life. Now remember, twice before, Delilah's plan had failed.

Playing on the Cliff of Your Life

But Samson is going to play again. He's going to make up some funny story and mock them again. You'd think he would be wise and say, "No, I'm on the edge of the cliff about to fall off. I need to be cautious here. I need to leave this woman. I need to leave this company and go and do what God has called me to do and stop messing around here in the camp of the world."

But it seemed good to him to have fun. You see, people have this idea that they can carry on in the world. They think they can carry on with ungodly relationships and ungodly acquaintances and it's fine. They say, "It's not having an affect in my life."

It might not have an affect on you now. But two or three years from today what type of person are you going to be? It might not show an affect in your life right now. But five years from now, where will you be?

Will you be more on fire for God five years from now? If you are less on fire for God than you were five years ago, then you need to change what you've been doing for the last five years and get to the place where you can stay on fire for God, full of the Holy Ghost, and walking in the Spirit.

And he said unto her, If they bind me fast with a new ropes that never were occupied, then shall I be weak, and be as another man.

> Delilah therefore took new ropes, and bound him therewith, and said unto him, The Philistines be upon thee, Samson. And there were liers in wait abiding in the chamber. And he brake them from off his arms like a thread.

> Judges 16:11, 12

Don't Touch Your Hair

> And Delilah said unto Samson, Hitherto thou hast mocked me, and told me lies: tell me wherewith thou mightest be bound. And he said unto her, If thou weavest the seven locks of my head with the web.

> Judges 16:13

I want you to see that Samson had begun to touch the very key to his anointing. He had played the other three times but now he was starting to touch the covering of the anointing of God on his life. He even mentioned part of the secret which was his hair.

He didn't tell them to shave him, but he told them to make seven locks of his hair and then to bind it up and fasten it. This is what Delilah did.

There were a lot of weavers in those days. They would weave carpets and clothing and all kinds of things. That's what Samson was saying. "Weave all my seven locks into the weaver's beam. Then I'll be weak." He didn't give the secret, but he was touching the very source of the anointing on his life.

> And she fastened it with the pin, and said unto him, The Philistines be upon thee, Samson. And he awaked out of his sleep, and went away with the pin of the beam, and with the web.
>
> And she said unto him, How canst thou say, I love thee, when thine heart is not with me? thou hast mocked me these three times, and hast not told me wherein thy great strength lieth.
>
> And it came to pass, when she pressed him daily with her words, and urged him, so that his soul was vexed unto death.
>
> **Judges 16:14-16**

She did what only a woman could do. It must have been hell on earth. Nag, nag, nag, nag, nag. Morning, noon, and night. "You don't love me."

It was so bad that his soul was vexed unto death. Samson wanted to die. That's how bad it was. This woman went on and on and on so that he wanted to die. He said, "My soul is vexed to death." Some women have that ability. She bugged him and bugged him, until he told her all his heart.

That's what the enemy wants to do. He wants to get you to a place where you open your heart and compromise the very deep things of God and lose your effectiveness for the Lord Jesus Christ.

I Said, Don't Touch Your Hair

Then he told her all his heart, and said unto her, There hath not come a rasor upon mine head; for I have been a Nazarite unto God from my mother's womb: if I be shaven, then my strength will go from me, and I shall become weak, and be like any other man.

And when Delilah saw that he had told her all his heart, she sent and called for the lords of the Philistines, saying, Come up this once, for he hath shewed me all his heart. Then the lords of the Philistines came up unto her, and brought money in their hand.

And she made him sleep upon her knees; and she called for a man, and she caused him to shave off the seven locks of his head; and she began to afflict him, and his strength went from him.

And she said, The Philistines be upon thee, Samson. And he awoke out of his sleep, and said, I will go out as at other times before and shake myself.

Judges 16:17-20

You see, Samson had reached the place where he thought even if they shaved his hair off, he was invincible. "I'm going to get up and shake myself and go out like I did the other times." That's what he thought.

And he wist not that the Lord was departed from him.

Judges 16:20

The Anointing Has Left and Some Don't Know It

Now, I want you to see something here. Samson lost the anointing and didn't know it. There are people today in churches who have lost the anointing and don't know it. They're deacons, elders, ministers, and congregation members who have lost the anointing and don't know it's gone.

That's a sad thing, that people who have had the anointing of God upon their lives can go into an area where they still think the anointing of God is on them, yet it's gone. That is one of the most dangerous places to be.

> But the Philistines took him, and put out his eyes, and brought him down to Gaza, and bound him with fetters of brass; and he did grind in the prison house.
>
> Howbeit the hair of his head began to grow again after it was shaven.
>
> **Judges 16:21, 22**

The Results of Losing the Anointing

The first thing that happened was Samson lost his covering; he lost his hair. And in losing his hair, he lost his strength. I believe he not only lost his hair, I believe he lost his joy. Because the Bible says the joy of the Lord is our strength. The hair of Samson was his strength. He lost his hair and he lost his strength. Here he is a bald, weak man.

The second thing that happened to him was that he lost his eyesight. They poked his eyes out and he lost his ability to see. When the anointing goes from you, you lose your ability to see into the Spirit. You're like a blind man stumbling around in a room.

You can't see clearly. You stumble around in darkness, crying, "O God, show me, show me." And there never comes an answer because you can't see.

Samson lost his eyesight. He lost the ability to see. He lost his freedom. They put him in captivity. They bound him with chains. Then they took him and made him do the work of a donkey. When you lose the anointing, you become like a donkey. His job was to grind the corn. How hard it becomes.

Doing the Work of a Donkey

When the anointing is not there, you go one more time around the mill. Your life becomes a grind and you are doing the work of a donkey. It becomes repetitious. There's no excitement, no joy, no strength. "I'm going round and round and round. I can't see like I used to. I don't have freedom like I used to."

When you lose the anointing, the world has the ability to mock at you and they're mocking at the Church right now. They're mocking at the house of God. They mock at men and women of God.

Anoint Me One More Time

Now the Philistines were having a feast. The world is having a feast right now. But at their time of reveling, at their time of feasting, will come their time of greatest defeat.

Guess what the Philistines did? They held a feast and said, "Bring this bald, blind man here. Let's mock him."

And in that moment of weakness, Samson remembered what was once upon his life and he prayed a prayer that would ultimately fulfill his ministry. But what a terrible way to fulfill your ministry. As he bowed himself there in that pagan temple, he pulled down its pillars. The whole place came down. In his death, he killed more than he did in his life.

Samson ultimately fulfilled his ministry. The anointing came back to him. But what a terrible way to find the ultimate fulfillment of God's call on your life.

Let's fulfill it with our eyes. Let's keep our hair on. And let's not put ourselves in the place of compromise.

Your "Delilah" could be your friends. Maybe you hang around with ungodly friends. Your "Delilah" could be something else. For everyone it is different. You must locate it and deal with it in your life before it kills you. Never let the devil steal the anointing from you. Do whatever it takes to keep the touch of God upon your life.

Anointing Scriptures

1. Anoint

And thou shalt put them upon Aaron thy brother, and his sons with him; and shalt anoint them, and consecrate them, and sanctify them, that they may minister unto me in the priest's office.

Exodus 28:41

Then shalt thou take the anointing oil, and pour it upon his head, and anoint him.

Exodus 29:7

And thou shalt offer every day a bullock for a sin offering for atonement: and thou shalt cleanse the altar, when thou hast made an atonement for it, and thou shalt anoint it, to sanctify it.

Exodus 29:36

And thou shalt anoint the tabernacle of the congregation therewith, and the ark of the testimony,

Exodus 30:26

And thou shalt anoint Aaron and his sons, and consecrate them, that they may minister unto me in the priest's office.

Exodus 30:30

And thou shalt take the anointing oil, and anoint the tabernacle, and all that is therein, and shalt hallow it, and all the vessels thereof: and it shall be holy.

Exodus 40:9

And thou shalt anoint the altar of the burnt offering, and all his vessels, and sanctify the altar: and it shall be an altar most holy.

Exodus 40:10

And thou shalt anoint the laver and his foot, and sanctify it.

Exodus 40:11

And thou shalt put upon Aaron the holy garments, and anoint him, and sanctify him; that he may minister unto me in the priest's office.

Exodus 40:13

And thou shalt anoint them, as thou didst anoint their father, that they may minister unto me in the priest's office: for their anointing shall surely be an everlasting priesthood throughout their generations.

Exodus 40:15

And the priest, whom he shall anoint, and whom he shall consecrate to minister in the priest's office in his father's stead, shall make the atonement, and shall put on the linen clothes, even the holy garments:

Leviticus 16:32

Thou shalt have olive trees throughout all thy coasts, but thou shalt not anoint thyself with the oil; for thine olive shall cast this fruit.

Deuteronomy 28:40

The trees went forth on a time to anoint a king over them; and they said unto the olive tree, Reign thou over us.

Judges 9:8

And the bramble said unto the trees, If in truth ye anoint me king over you, then come and put your trust in my shadow: and if not, let fire come out of the bramble, and devour the cedars of Lebanon.

Judges 9:15

Wash thyself therefore, and anoint thee, and put thy raiment upon thee, and get thee down to the floor: but make not thyself known unto the man, until he shall have done eating and drinking.

Ruth 3:3

Tomorrow about this time I will send thee a man out of the land of Benjamin, and thou shalt anoint him to be captain over my people Israel, that he may save my people out of the hand of the Philistines: for I have looked upon my people, because their cry is come unto me.

1 Samuel 9:16

Samuel also said unto Saul, The Lord sent me to anoint thee to be king over his people, over Israel: now therefore hearken thou unto the voice of the words of the Lord.

1 Samuel 15:1

And call Jesse to the sacrifice, and I will shew thee what thou shalt do: and thou shalt anoint unto me him whom I name unto thee.

1 Samuel 16:3

And he sent, and brought him in. Now he was ruddy, and withal of a beautiful countenance, and goodly to look to. And the Lord said, Arise, anoint him: for this is he.

1 Samuel 16:12

And Joab sent to Tekoah, and fetched thence a wise woman, and said unto her, I pray thee, feign thyself to be a mourner, and put on now mourning apparel, and anoint not thyself with oil, but be as a woman that had a long time mourned for the dead:

2 Samuel 14:2

And let Zadok the priest and Nathan the prophet anoint him there king over Israel: and blow ye with the trumpet, and say, God save king Solomon.

1 Kings 1:34

And the Lord said unto him, Go, return on thy way to the wilderness of Damascus: and when thou comest, anoint Hazael to be king over Syria:

1 Kings 19:15

And Jehu the son of Nimshi shalt thou anoint to be king over Israel: and Elisha the son of Shaphat of Abelmeholah shalt thou anoint to be prophet in thy room.

1 Kings 19:16

Prepare the table, watch in the watchtower, eat, drink: arise, ye princes, and anoint the shield.

Isaiah 21:5

Seventy weeks are determined upon thy people and upon thy holy city, to finish the transgression, and to make an end of sins, and to make reconciliation for iniquity, and to bring in everlasting righteousness, and to seal up the vision and prophecy, and to anoint the most Holy.

Daniel 9:24

I ate no pleasant bread, neither came flesh nor wine in my mouth, neither did I anoint myself at all, till three whole weeks were fulfilled.

Daniel 10:3

That drink wine in bowls, and anoint themselves with the chief ointments: but they are not grieved for the affliction of Joseph.

Amos 6:6

Thou shalt sow, but thou shalt not reap; thou shalt tread the olives, but thou shalt not anoint thee with oil; and sweet wine, but shalt not drink wine.

Micah 6:15

But thou, when thou fastest, anoint thine head, and wash thy face;

Matthew 6:17

She hath done what she could: she is come aforehand to anoint my body to the burying.

Mark 14:8

And when the sabbath was past, Mary Magdalene, and Mary the mother of James, and Salome, had bought sweet spices, that they might come and anoint him.

Mark 16:1

My head with oil thou didst not anoint: but this woman hath anointed my feet with ointment.

Luke 7:46

I counsel thee to buy of me gold tried in the fire, that thou mayest be rich; and white raiment, that thou mayest be clothed, and that the shame of thy nakedness do not appear; and anoint thine eyes with eyesalve, that thou mayest see.

Revelations 3:18

2. Anointed

And unleavened bread, and cakes unleavened tempered with oil, and wafers unleavened anointed with oil: of wheaten flour shalt thou make them.

Exodus 29:2

And the holy garments of Aaron shall be his sons' after him, to be anointed therein, and to be consecrated in them.

Exodus 29:29

And if thou bring an oblation of a meat offering baken in the oven, it shall be unleavened cakes of fine flour mingled with oil, or unleavened wafers anointed with oil.

Leviticus 2:4

If the priest that is anointed do sin according to the sin of the people; then let him bring for his sin, which he hath sinned, a young bullock without blemish unto the Lord for a sin offering.

Leviticus 4:3

And the priest that is anointed shall take of the bullock's blood, and bring it to the tabernacle of the congregation:

Leviticus 4:5

And the priest that is anointed shall bring of the bullock's blood to the tabernacle of the congregation:

Leviticus 4:16

This is the offering of Aaron and of his sons, which they shall offer unto the Lord in the day when he is anointed; the tenth part of an ephah of fine flour for a meat offering perpetual, half of it in the morning, and half thereof at night.

Leviticus 6:20

And the priest of his sons that is anointed in his stead shall offer it: it is a statute for ever unto the Lord; it shall be wholly burnt.

Leviticus 6:22

If he offer it for a thanksgiving, then he shall offer with the sacrifice of thanksgiving unleavened cakes mingled with oil, and unleavened wafers anointed with oil, and cakes mingled with oil, of fine flour, fried.

Leviticus 7:12

Which the Lord commanded to be given them of the children of Israel, in the day that he anointed them, by a statute for ever throughout their generations.

Leviticus 7:36

And Moses took the anointing oil, and anointed the tabernacle and all that was therein, and sanctified them.

Leviticus 8:10

And he sprinkled thereof upon the altar seven times, and anointed the altar and all his vessels, both the laver and his foot, to sanctify them.

Leviticus 8:11

And he poured of the anointing oil upon Aaron's head, and anointed him, to sanctify him.

Leviticus 8:12

These are the names of the sons of Aaron, the priests which were anointed, whom he consecrated to minister in the priest's office.

Numbers 3:3

And a basket of unleavened bread, cakes of fine flour mingled with oil, and wafers of unleavened bread anointed with oil, and their meat offering, and their drink offerings.

Numbers 6:15

And it came to pass on the day that Moses had fully set up the tabernacle, and had anointed it, and sanctified it, and all the instruments thereof, both the altar and all the vessels thereof, and had anointed them, and sanctified them;

Numbers 7:1

And the princes offered for dedicating of the altar in the day that it was anointed, even the princes offered their offering before the altar.

Numbers 7:10

This was the dedication of the altar, in the day when it was anointed, by the princes of Israel: twelve chargers of silver, twelve silver bowls, twelve spoons of gold:

Numbers 7:84

And all the oxen for the sacrifice of the peace offerings were twenty and four bullocks, the rams sixty, the he goats sixty, the lambs of the first year sixty. This was the dedication of the altar, after that it was anointed.

Numbers 7:88

And the congregation shall deliver the slayer out of the
hand of the revenger of blood, and the congregation shall
restore him to the city of his refuge, whither he was fled:
and he shall abide in it unto the death of the high priest,
which was anointed with the holy oil.

Numbers 35:25

The adversaries of the Lord shall be broken to pieces;
out of heaven shall he thunder upon them: the Lord shall
judge the ends of the earth; and he shall give strength unto
his king, and exalt the horn of his anointed.

1 Samuel 2:10

And I will raise me up a faithful priest, that shall do
according to that which is in mine heart and in my mind:
and I will build him a sure house; and he shall walk before
mine anointed for ever.

1 Samuel 2:35

Then Samuel took a vial of oil, and poured it upon his
head, and kissed him, and said, Is it not because the Lord
hath anointed thee to be captain over his inheritance?

1 Samuel 10:1

Behold, here I am: witness against me before the Lord,
and before his anointed: whose ox have I taken? or whose
ass have I taken? or whom have I defrauded? whom have I
oppressed? or of whose hand have I received any bribe to
blind mine eyes therewith? and I will restore it you.

1 Samuel 12:3

And he said unto them, The Lord is witness against you,
and his anointed is witness this day, that ye have not found
ought in my hand. And they answered, He is witness.

1 Samuel 12:5

And Samuel said, When thou wast little in thine own
sight, wast thou not made the head of the tribes of Israel,
and the Lord anointed thee king over Israel?

1 Samuel 15:17

And it came to pass, when they were come, that he looked on Eliab, and said, Surely the Lord's anointed is before him.

1 Samuel 16:6

Then Samuel took the horn of oil, and anointed him in the midst of his brethren: and the Spirit of the Lord came upon David from that day forward. So Samuel rose up, and went to Ramah.

1 Samuel 16:13

And he said unto his men, The Lord forbid that I should do this thing unto my master, the Lord's anointed, to stretch forth mine hand against him, seeing he is the anointed of the Lord.

1 Samuel 24:6

Behold, this day thine eyes have seen how that the Lord had delivered thee to day into mine hand in the cave: and some bade me kill thee: but mine eye spared thee; and I said, I will not put forth mine hand against my lord; for he is the Lord's anointed.

1 Samuel 24:10

And David said to Abishai, Destroy him not: for who can stretch forth his hand against the Lord's anointed, and be guiltless?

1 Samuel 26:9

The Lord forbid that I should stretch forth mine hand against the Lord's anointed: but, I pray thee, take thou now the spear that is at his bolster, and the cruse of water, and let us go.

1 Samuel 26:11

This thing is not good that thou hast done. As the Lord liveth, ye are worthy to die, because ye have not kept your master, the Lord's anointed. And now see where the king's spear is, and the cruse of water that was at his bolster.

1 Samuel 26:16

The Lord render to every man his righteousness and his faithfulness: for the Lord delivered thee into my hand to day, but I would not stretch forth mine hand against the Lord's anointed.

1 Samuel 26:23

And David said unto him, How wast thou not afraid to stretch forth thine hand to destroy the Lord's anointed?

2 Samuel 1:14

And David said unto him, Thy blood be upon thy head; for thy mouth hath testified against thee, saying, I have slain the Lord's anointed.

2 Samuel 1:16

Ye mountains of Gilboa, let there be no dew, neither let there be rain, upon you, nor fields of offerings: for there the shield of the mighty is vilely cast away, the shield of Saul, as though he had not been anointed with oil.

2 Samuel 1:21

And the men of Judah came, and there they anointed David king over the house of Judah. And they told David, saying, That the men of Jabesh-gilead were they that buried Saul.

2 Samuel 2:4

Therefore now let your hands be strengthened, and be ye valiant: for your master Saul is dead, and also the house of Judah have anointed me king over them.

2 Samuel 2:7

And I am this day weak, though anointed king; and these men the sons of Zeruiah be too hard for me: the Lord shall reward the doer of evil according to his wickedness.

2 Samuel 3:39

So all the elders of Israel came to the king to Hebron; and king David made a league with them in Hebron before the Lord: and they anointed David king over Israel.

2 Samuel 5:3

But when the Philistines heard that they had anointed David king over Israel, all the Philistines came up to seek David; and David heard of it, and went down to the hold.

2 Samuel 5:17

And Nathan said to David, Thou art the man. Thus saith the Lord God of Israel, I anointed thee king over Israel, and I delivered thee out of the hand of Saul;

2 Samuel 12:7

Then David arose from the earth, and washed, and anointed himself, and changed his apparel, and came into the house of the Lord, and worshipped: then he came to his own house; and when he required,they set bread before him, and he did eat.

2 Samuel 12:20

And Absalom, whom we anointed over us, is dead in battle. Now therefore why speak ye not a word of bringing the king back?

2 Samuel 19:10

But Abishai the son of Zeruiah answered and said, Shall not Shimei be put to death for this, because he cursed the Lord's anointed?

2 Samuel 19:21

He is the tower of salvation for his king: and sheweth mercy to his anointed, unto David, and to his seed for evermore.

2 Samuel 22:51

Now these be the last words of David. David the son of Jesse said, and the man who was raised up on high, the anointed of the God of Jacob, and the sweet psalmist of Israel, said,

2 Samuel 23:1

And Zadok the priest took an horn of oil out of the tabernacle, and anointed Solomon. And they blew the trumpet; and all the people said, God save king Solomon.

1 Kings 1:39

And Zadok the priest and Nathan the prophet have anointed him king in Gihon: and they are come up from thence rejoicing, so that the city rang again. This is the noise that ye have heard.

1 Kings 1:45

And Hiram king of Tyre sent his servants unto Solomon; for he had heard that they had anointed him king in the room of his father: for Hiram was ever a lover of David.

1 Kings 5:1

Then take the box of oil, and pour it on his head, and say, Thus saith the Lord, I have anointed thee king over Israel. Then open the door, and flee, and tarry not.

2 Kings 9:3

And he arose, and went into the house; and he poured the oil on his head, and said unto him, Thus saith the Lord God of Israel, I have anointed thee king over the people of the Lord, even over Israel.

2 Kings 9:6

And they said, It is false; tell us now. And he said, Thus and thus spake he to me, saying, Thus saith the Lord, I have anointed thee king over Israel.

2 Kings 9:12

And he brought forth the king's son, and put the crown upon him, and gave him the testimony; and they made him king, and anointed him; and they clapped their hands, and said, God save the king.

2 Kings 11:12

And his servants carried him in a chariot dead from Megiddo, and brought him to Jerusalem, and buried him in his own sepulchre. And the people of the land took Jehoahaz the son of Josiah, and anointed him, and made him king in his father's stead.

2 King 23:30

Therefore came all the elders of Israel to the king to Hebron; and David made a covenant with them in Hebron before the Lord; and they anointed David king over Israel, according to the word of the Lord by Samuel.

1 Chronicles 11:3

And when the Philistines heard that David was anointed king over all Israel, all the Philistines went up to seek David. And David heard of it, and went out against them.

1 Chronicles 14:8

Saying, Touch not mine anointed, and do my prophets no harm.

1 Chronicles 16:22

And did eat and drink before the Lord on that day with great gladness. And they made Solomon the son of David king the second time, and anointed him unto the Lord to be the chief governor, and Zadok to be priest.

1 Chronicles 29:22

O Lord God, turn not away the face of thine anointed: remember the mercies of David thy servant.

2 Chronicles 6:42

And the destruction of Ahaziah was of God by coming to Joram: for when he was come, he went out with Jehoram against Jehu the son of Nimshi, whom the Lord had anointed to cut off the house of Ahab.

2 Chronicles 22:7

Then they brought out the king's son, and put upon him the crown, and gave him the testimony, and made him king. And Jehoiada and his sons anointed him, and said, God save the king.

2 Chronicles 23:11

And the men which were expressed by name rose up, and took the captives, and with the spoil clothed all that were naked among them, and arrayed them, and shod them, and gave them to eat and to drink, and anointed them, and carried all the feeble of them upon asses, and brought them to Jericho, the city of palm trees, to their brethren: then they returned to Samaria.

2 Chronicles 28:15

The kings of the earth set themselves, and the rulers take counsel together, against the Lord, and against his anointed, saying,

Psalm 2:2

Great deliverance giveth he to his king; and sheweth mercy to his anointed, to David, and to his seed for evermore.

Psalm 18:50

Now know I that the Lord saveth his anointed; he will hear him from his holy heaven with the saving strength of his right hand.

Psalm 20:6

The Lord is their strength, and he is the saving strength of his anointed.

Psalm 28:8

Thou lovest righteousness, and hatest wickedness: therefore God, thy God, hath anointed thee with the oil of gladness above thy fellows.

Psalm 45:7

Behold, O God our shield, and look upon the face of thine anointed.

Psalm 84:9

I have found David my servant; with my holy oil have I anointed him:

Psalm 89:20

But thou hast cast off and abhorred, thou hast been wroth with thine anointed.

Psalm 89:38

Wherewith thine enemies have reproached, O Lord; wherewith they have reproached the footsteps of thine anointed.

Psalm 89:51

But my horn shalt thou exalt like the horn of an unicorn: I shall be anointed with fresh oil.

Psalm 92:10

Saying, Touch not mine anointed, and do my prophets no harm.

Psalm 105:15

For thy servant David's sake turn not away the face of thine anointed.

Psalm 132:10

There will I make the horn of David to bud: I have ordained a lamp for mine anointed.

Psalm 132:17

Thus saith the Lord to his anointed, to Cyrus, whose right hand I have holden, to subdue nations before him; and I will loose the loins of kings, to open before him the two leaved gates; and the gates shall not be shut;

Isaiah 45:1

The Spirit of the Lord God is upon me; because the Lord hath anointed me to preach good tidings unto the meek; he hath sent me to bind up the brokenhearted, to proclaim liberty to the captives, and the opening of the prison to them that are bound;

Isaiah 61:1

The breath of our nostrils, the anointed of the Lord, was taken in their pits, of whom we said, Under his shadow we shall live among the heathen.

Lamentations 4:20

Then washed I thee with water; yea, I thoroughly washed away thy blood from thee, and I anointed thee with oil.

Ezekiel 16:9

Thou art the anointed cherub that covereth; and I have set thee so: thou wast upon the holy mountain of God; thou hast walked up and down in the midst of the stones of fire.

Ezekiel 28:14

Thou wentest forth for the salvation of thy people, even for salvation with thine anointed; thou woundedst the head out of the house of the wicked, by discovering the foundation unto the neck. Selah.

Habakkuk 3:13

Then said he, These are the two anointed ones, that stand by the Lord of the whole earth.

Zechariah 4:14

And they cast out many devils, and anointed with oil many that were sick, and healed them.

Mark 6:13

The Spirit of the Lord is upon me, because he hath anointed me to preach the gospel to the poor; he hath sent me to heal the brokenhearted, to preach deliverance to the captives, and recovering of sight to the blind, to set at liberty them that are bruised,

Luke 4:18

And stood at his feet behind him weeping, and began to wash his feet with tears, and did wipe them with the hairs of her head, and kissed his feet, and anointed them with the ointment.

Luke 7:38

My head with oil thou didst not anoint: but this woman hath anointed my feet with ointment.

Luke 7:46

When he had thus spoken, he spat on the ground, and made clay of the spittle, and he anointed the eyes of the blind man with the clay,

John 9:6

He answered and said, A man that is called Jesus made clay, and anointed mine eyes, and said unto me, Go to the pool of Siloam, and wash: and I went and washed, and I received sight.

John 9:11

(It was that Mary which anointed the Lord with ointment, and wiped his feet with her hair, whose brother Lazarus was sick.)

John 11:2

Then took Mary a pound of ointment of spikenard, very costly, and anointed the feet of Jesus, and wiped his feet with her hair: and the house was filled with the odour of the ointment.

John 12:3

For of a truth against thy holy child Jesus, whom thou hast anointed, both Herod, and Pontius Pilate, with the Gentiles, and the people of Israel, were gathered together,

Acts 4:27

How God anointed Jesus of Nazareth with the Holy Ghost and with power: who went about doing good, and healing all that were oppressed of the devil; for God was with him.

Acts 10:38

Now he which stablisheth us with you in Christ, and hath anointed us, is God;

2 Corinthians 1:21

Thou hast loved righteousness, and hated iniquity; therefore God, even thy God, hath anointed thee with the oil of gladness above thy fellows.

Hebrews 1:9

3. Anointing

Oil for the light, spices for anointing oil, and for sweet incense,

Exodus 25:6

Then shalt thou take the anointing oil, and pour it upon his head, and anoint him.

Exodus 29:7

And thou shalt take of the blood that is upon the altar, and of the anointing oil, and sprinkle it upon Aaron, and upon his garments, and upon his sons, and upon the garments of his sons with him: and he shall be hallowed, and his garments, and his sons, and his sons' garments with him.

Exodus 29:21

And thou shalt make it an oil of holy ointment, an ointment compound after the art of the apothecary: it shall be an holy anointing oil.

Exodus 30:25

And thou shalt speak unto the children of Israel, saying, This shall be an holy anointing oil unto me throughout your generations.

Exodus 30:31

And the anointing oil, and sweet incense for the holy place: according to all that I have commanded thee shall they do.

Exodus 31:11

And oil for the light, and spices for anointing oil, and for the sweet incense,

Exodus 35:8

And the incense altar, and his staves, and the anointing oil, and the sweet incense, and the hanging for the door at the entering in of the tabernacle,

Exodus 35:15

And spice, and oil for the light, and for the anointing oil, and for the sweet incense.

Exodus 35:28

And he made the holy anointing oil, and the pure incense of sweet spices, according to the work of the apothecary.

Exodus 37:29

And the golden altar, and the anointing oil, and the sweet incense, and the hanging for the tabernacle door,

Exodus 39:38

And thou shalt take the anointing oil, and anoint the tabernacle, and all that is therein, and shalt hallow it, and all the vessels thereof: and it shall be holy.

Exodus 40:9

And thou shalt anoint them, as thou didst anoint their father, that they may minister unto me in the priest's office: for their anointing shall surely be an everlasting priesthood throughout their generations.

Exodus 40:15

This is the portion of the anointing of Aaron, and of the anointing of his sons, out of the offerings of the Lord made by fire, in the day when he presented them to minister unto the Lord in the priest's office;

Leviticus 7:35

Take Aaron and his sons with him, and the garments, and the anointing oil, and a bullock for the sin offering, and two rams, and a basket of unleavened bread;

Leviticus 8:2

And Moses took the anointing oil, and anointed the tabernacle and all that was therein, and sanctified them.

Leviticus 8:10

And he poured of the anointing oil upon Aaron's head, and anointed him, to sanctify him.

Leviticus 8:12

And Moses took of the anointing oil, and of the blood which was upon the altar, and sprinkled it upon Aaron, and upon his garments, and upon his sons, and upon his sons' garments with him; and sanctified Aaron, and his garments, and his sons, and his sons' garments with him.

Leviticus 8:30

And ye shall not go out from the door of the tabernacle of the congregation, lest ye die: for the anointing oil of the Lord is upon you. And they did according to the word of Moses.

Leviticus 10:7

And he that is the high priest among his brethren, upon whose head the anointing oil was poured, and that is consecrated to put on the garments, shall not uncover his head, nor rend his clothes;

Leviticus 21:10

Neither shall he go out of the sanctuary, nor profane the sanctuary of his God; for the crown of the anointing oil of his God is upon him: I am the Lord.

Leviticus 21:12

And to the office of Eleazar the son of Aaron the priest pertaineth the oil for the light, and the sweet incense, and the daily meat offering, and the anointing oil, and the oversight of all the tabernacle, and of all that therein is, in the sanctuary, and in the vessels thereof.

Numbers 4:16

And the Lord spake unto Aaron, Behold, I also have given thee the charge of mine heave offerings of all the hallowed things of the children of Israel; unto thee have I given them by reason of the anointing, and to thy sons, by an ordinance for ever.

Numbers 18:8

And it shall come to pass in that day, that his burden shall be taken away from off thy shoulder, and his yoke from off thy neck, and the yoke shall be destroyed because of the anointing.

Isaiah 10:27

Is any sick among you? let him call for the elders of the church; and let them pray over him, anointing him with oil in the name of the Lord:

James 5:14

But the anointing which ye have received of him abideth in you, and ye need not that any man teach you: but as the same anointing teacheth you of all things, and is truth, and is no lie, and even as it hath taught you, ye shall abide in him.

1 John 2:27

Postscript

I feel that I would like to add a postscript to this book to encourage the reader, that if you have been blessed by this book and challenged, to please write to me at my Louisville office or call me. We would love to hear from you. If you were stirred and challenged to change, I pray that God would use you in a wonderful way to touch a lost and dying world.

Write:
Rodney Howard-Browne
Evangelistic Association Inc.
P.O. Box 197161
Louisville, Kentucky 40259
Telephone: 1-800-354-6880

Other Book titles available are:
Flowing in the Holy Ghost
A Practical Handbook on the Gifts.

Mini-book titles available are:
Manifesting the Holy Ghost
The Reality of the Person of the Holy Spirit
Fresh Oil From Heaven
The Anointing
The Coming revival
Walking in the Perfect Will of God
What it Means to be Born Again

Videos available are:
Manifesting the Holy Ghost
The Hand of the Lord
Flowing in the Holy Ghost
The Touch of God
The Reality of the Person of the Holy Spirit
The Coming Revival

Tape series available are:
Flowing in the Holy Ghost
The Touch of God

Personal Notes

Personal Notes

Personal Notes

Personal Notes

Personal Notes

Personal Notes

Personal Notes

Personal Notes

Personal Notes

Personal Notes

Personal Notes